D1246858

TRADE PREFERENCES FOR DEVELOPING COUNTRIES

PROBLEMS OF ECONOMIC INTEGRATION

General Editor: GEORGE W. MCKENZIE

PUBLISHED

European Industrial Organisation
Alexis P. Jacquemin, University of Louvain, and Henry W. de Jong,
  Netherlands School of Business

The Economics of the Euro-Currency System
George W. McKenzie, University of Southampton

Trade Preferences for Developing Countries
Tracy Murray, Graduate School of Business Administration, New York
  University

International Economics of Pollution
Ingo Walter, Graduate School of Business Administration, New York
  University

FORTHCOMING

Economic Interdependence
Sven W. Arndt, University of California at Santa Cruz

International Capital Flows
David T. Llewellyn, University of Nottingham

Trade Preferences for Developing Countries

TRACY MURRAY
Graduate School of Business Administration
New York University

A HALSTED PRESS BOOK

JOHN WILEY & SONS
New York – Toronto

© Tracy Murray 1977

First published in Great Britain 1977 by
The Macmillan Press Ltd

Published in the U.S.A. and
Canada by Halsted Press, a
Division of John Wiley & Sons, Inc.
New York

Printed in Great Britain

Library of Congress Cataloging in Publication Data

Murray, Tracy.
    Trade preferences for developing countries.

    (Problems of economic integration)
    "A Halsted Press book."
    Bibliography: p.
    Includes index.
    1. Tariff preferences. 2. Underdeveloped areas—
Tariff. 3. Underdeveloped areas—Commerce. I. Title.
HF1721.M87   1977   382.7   76–58546
ISBN 0 470–99080–5

Dedicated to
Kathi, Lisa and Scott

Contents

General Editor's Preface

Since the Second World War, the economies of Europe, North America, Japan and the developing world have become increasingly interdependent. This has taken place at various levels. On the one hand we have seen the formation and growth of a formal organisation, the European Economic Community, whose aim it is to strengthen existing political and economic ties amongst its members. But interdependence is not solely the result of legal treaties; it is also the outcome of economic innovation and evolution. The growth of the multinational corporation, the development of the euro-currency system and the rapid growth of international trade are but examples of the trend.

Yet the resulting closer ties among nations have been a mixed blessing. It is no longer possible for governments to formulate national objectives in isolation from activity in the rest of the world. Monetary, fiscal, antitrust and social policies now have widespread implications beyond national frontiers. How to cope with the complex implications of the current petroleum price developments is but an example of the sort of problem arising in an inter-dependent world.

Despite its obvious importance most economics textbooks give only cursory attention to international economic interdependence. The purpose of this series is to fill this gap by providing critical surveys and analyses of specific types of economic linkages among nations. It is thus hoped that the volumes will appeal not only to students, researchers and government bodies working in the field of international economics but also to those dealing with the problems of industrial organisation, monetary economics and other aspects of public policy which have traditionally been studied from a narrow, nationalistic viewpoint.

Department of Economics
Southampton University

GEORGE W. McKENZIE

Preface

I first became interested in the subject of trade preferences for developing countries when I joined the staff of the U.N. Conference on Trade and Development (UNCTAD) in Geneva during a two-year leave of absence from my academic post. I arrived on the scene on 30 June 1971, one day prior to the introduction of the first system of preferential tariffs by the European Economic Community. During the following two years, ten additional schemes were introduced by industrial countries of the West; Canada followed in 1974 and the United States completed the entire system on 1 January 1976. During my tenure with UNCTAD I had an opportunity to learn the intimate details of the entire system – the politics behind the institutional features of each preference scheme, the economic advantages sought by the developing countries, and the trade impediments resulting from various limitations contained in the regulations governing preferential trading. To say the least, it was a very interesting, illuminating and at the same time frustrating experience.

At the Secretariat I was charged with conducting economic studies to evaluate various aspects of the system. These studies showed quite convincingly that the trade benefits for developing countries were likely to be quite meagre. As a pseudo-outsider, I soon became the Secretariat's most vocal critic of the generalised system of preferences (G.S.P.). My colleagues, however, were much more hopeful that the system would some day amount to something worth while. They recognised that changes in international institutions come very slowly, that initial steps for change are taken with extreme caution, and that only after the implications of the first steps are known and evaluated will further and more meaningful steps be taken. By the end of my two-year stay I was more sympathetic to their point of view – though still a critic of the system as it then existed. But I was hopeful that the preference system would be improved and that meaningful trade benefits for the developing countries would be realised. However, the ensuing events since my return to academia have led me to become more sceptical as no meaningful improvements have been made; and in the meantime other events may so alter the institutions governing international trade that any future improvements in the G.S.P. will amount to too little too late.

THE PLAN OF THE BOOK

The story of *Trade Preference for Developing Countries* is told in three parts. Part 1 discusses the origin of the concept of trade preferences for development, the political problems in negotiating such a drastic change in the rules governing international trade, and an economic analysis of the impact which trade preferences would have on developing-country exports. Part 2 examines the operation and effects of the preference system which was actually introduced. As Part 1 reveals, the actual system differed quite significantly from that which was envisaged by the developing countries. As a consequence, the trade benefits fall far short of what was initially expected. Finally, in Part 3 the trade preferences are put in perspective. It is noted that the rules governing international trade are going through a rapidly evolving period which will affect the advantages to be gained from tariff preferences. Those changes which are likely to have the largest impact on the system include: the enlargement of the European Community and the revision in its trading arrangements with numerous developing countries; the formation of a new West European free-trade area; the new round of trade negotiations under the auspices of GATT; and finally, the new initiatives taken by the developing countries aiming at a so-called 'New International Economic Order'.

ACKNOWLEDGMENTS

This book is the outgrowth of a number of articles and U.N. documents which I have authored or co-authored on the generalised system of preferences (G.S.P.). In addition, I have drawn liberally on the works and ideas of others. Since I do not consider this to be an original work, but instead an up-to-date synthesis of what is known, I have attempted to minimise the number of interruptions in the text by omitting source citations for many of the points discussed. Instead I prefer to acknowledge the most important of my many intellectual debts here.

Probably the two most important volumes on the trade problems and policies regarding developing countries are *Towards a New Trade Policy for Development* (the so-called 'Prebisch Report' to the 1964 U.N. Conference on Trade and Development) and Professor H. G. Johnson's *Economic Policies Toward Less Developed Countries* (Brookings Institution, 1967). My use of arguments from these two volumes is most obvious in Part 1.

Numerous UNCTAD Secretariat personnel had a major impact on the development of the ideas and evidence contained in this book. To name only a few, Mr. R. Krishnamurti, Mr. H. Stordel and Mr. J. Brandenburg of the Manufactures Division provided my education into the political workings of UNCTAD negotiations. This education sometimes came as the result of somewhat heated arguments during meetings to discuss final revisions in

U.N. documents which I had drafted – only later was I to fully understand and appreciate the political value of their criticisms.

My greatest debt is to Mr G. Tadić, Chief of the Preferences Section, who patiently forced me to carefully (and repeatedly) study the G.S.P. rules and regulations and who became the most rigorous and helpful reviewer that any author can hope to have, and Mr Abdelhak Belkora, an UNCTAD colleague and friend with whom I discussed and rediscussed nearly every idea presented in this book. In addition, I wish to thank Mr Benelmouffok, the fourth member of the UNCTAD G.S.P. team during my tenure.

Those who know the UNCTAD Secretariat understand the tremendous assistance provided by the computer and research support staff. I wish to single out Mr J. Gregory, Mrs M. Talbot and Miss S. Glangeaud, who were of immeasurable value to me.

During my term with UNCTAD I also had the opportunity to confer with numerous officials of various governmental missions to the United Nations in Geneva, and with numerous officials of the Government of Japan in Tokyo, the European Commission in Brussels and the U.S. Government in Washington. In the main, these officials were polite and informative. Occasionally there were those whose assistance went beyond normal protocol; Mr D. Dunford of the U.S. Department of State and Mr T. Graham of the U.S. Office of the Special Representative for Trade Negotiations must be especially thanked.

Academic colleagues whose encouragement and council deserve mention include Professors M. Kreinin and I. Walter; also thanks should go to J. M. Finger of the U.S. Department of Treasury and J. Tumlir and R. Blackhurst of the GATT Secretariat. Last but not least, in fact most, a special debt is owed to my co-authors, Professor Robert E. Baldwin and Peter J. Ginman (formerly Professor and now with the UNCTAD Secretariat), both of whom have graciously consented to have our joint work incorporated into this book.

Nor can I overlook the careful attention provided by my editor, Professor George McKenzie, and, of course, my secretary, Gayle Stafford. Financial support was provided in part by New York University summer research grants, by the New York University project on the 'Multinational Corporation in the U.S. and World Economy' and by an I.B.M. Post-Doctoral Fellowship for Studies in International Business.

Data and arguments from the following published works are incorporated; I thank the publishers for permission to use these materials.

Robert E. Baldwin and Tracy Murray, 'MFN Tariff Reductions and Developing Country Trade Benefits Under the GSP', *Economic Journal*, Mar 1977.

Peter J. Ginman and Tracy Murray, 'The Generalized System of Preferences: A Review and Appraisal', in *The New International Economic*

Order: Confrontation or Cooperation Between North and South?, ed. K. Sauvant and H. Hasenpflug (Boulder, Colorado: Westview Press, 1977).

Tracy Murray, 'GSP: What You Should Know', *International Trade Forum*, UNCTAD/GATT International Trade Centre, July–Sept 1972.

———— 'How Helpful is the Generalized System of Preferences to Developing Countries', *Economic Journal*, June 1973.

———— 'Preferential Tariffs for the LDCs', *Southern Economic Journal*, July 1973.

———— 'UNCTAD's Generalized Preferences: An Appraisal', *Journal of World Trade Law*, July/Aug 1973.

———— 'E.E.C. Enlargement and Preferences for the Developing Countries', *Economic Journal*, Sep 1973.

New York University   TRACY MURRAY
September 1976

PART 1

Introduction

Introduction to Part 1

Commencing in 1971, the long-awaited generalised system of preferences (G.S.P.) was introduced by a number of industrial nations, including Australia, Austria, Canada, the European Community (E.E.C. – Belgium, Denmark, France, Germany, Italy, Ireland, Luxembourg, the Netherlands and the United Kingdom), Finland, Japan, New Zealand, Norway, Sweden, Switzerland and the United States. Under the G.S.P. tariffs charged on imports of manufactured and semi-manufactured products from the developing countries are granted preferential tariff reductions in comparison with the most-favoured-nation (M.F.N.) duties charged on imports from other sources. The objective of this new system was to establish new international trade incentives that would contribute to raising the material wealth of the developing countries through trade rather than aid.

This new trade initiative was introduced some seven years after its first serious suggestion in 1964 at the U.N. Conference on Trade and Development (UNCTAD). Chapter 1 describes the various issues and conflicts underlying the intervening negotiations between the more than one hundred developing countries and the preference-giving developed countries. Starting from a trade system stacked against them, and the failures of GATT negotiations to redress these imbalances, it is not surprising that the developing countries in unison turned their attention toward the U.N. forum to negotiate a new system. The North–South negotiation process was thoroughly complicated by other issues such as East–West relations, U.S.–E.E.C.–Japan conflicts and industrial country protectionist pressures which run rampant during recessionary periods.

Chapter 2 examines the expected economic impact of tariff preferences on developing-country exports and development, noting the importance of manufacturing activities for improving living standards. Due to the escalated nature of tariff structures in the industrial countries, nevertheless the relatively low tariffs on manufactured products have a significant impact in discouraging industrial processing in developing countries.

1

The Generalised System of Preferences: Evolution from Concept to Fact

One of the most original new initiatives in the field of international trade policy aimed at stimulating economic development is the concept of preferential treatment in favour of the developing countries. In a strict sense the concept is not new, as the industrial centre has historically devoted special attention to the periphery especially under colonial-type arrangements. Grants in AID and concessionary development loans are other examples. However, the new initiative takes a non-traditional approach by granting exports from developing countries preferential access to the markets of the industrial centre, i.e. these preferential arrangements constitute a 'trade' policy rather than a more traditional 'AID' policy.

The idea for this new initiative was formally introduced at the U.N. Conference on Trade and Development (hereafter referred to as UNCTAD) when it first convened in Geneva in 1964. The goal of this conference was to establish a new international trade policy that would contribute to raising the material wealth of the developing countries through trade rather than aid. However, the results can hardly be called a great success for the developing countries as no substantive trade measures emerged.

Nevertheless, as a result of this conference the U.N. General Assembly, in Resolution 1995 (XIX), dated 30 December 1964, established UNCTAD as a permanent organ of the General Assembly.

UNCTAD provided an on-going forum for publicising the trade problems of the developing countries. And in 1968 when the second conference convened in New Delhi, the principle of generalised tariff preferences was formally accepted in Resolution 21 (II). This resolution also established the Special Committee on Preferences to negotiate the implementation of the Generalised System of Preferences (G.S.P.). On 14 November 1969 the developed countries belonging to the Organisation for Economic Co-operation and Development (O.E.C.D.) submitted their preference 'offers' to the developing countries through the Secretary-General of UNCTAD. Further negotiations ensued as these offers were revised and refined. Finally, on 1 July 1971 the E.E.C. of six member states implemented the first preferential tariff 'scheme'.* Soon after, preference schemes were also implemented by Japan (August 1971); Norway (October 1971); Denmark, Finland, Ireland,

---

* In fact, Australia introduced the first preferential tariff system in 1965, which was more limited and independent of the UNCTAD negotiations.

New Zealand, Sweden and the United Kingdom (January 1972);* Switzerland (March 1972) and Austria (April 1972). The developing countries had
to wait substantially longer for preferences from the remaining industrial
nations of the West, Canada, and the United States, who finally implemented their schemes in July 1974 and January 1976, respectively.†

TRADE PROBLEMS OF THE DEVELOPING COUNTRIES

The present structure of world trade is in part one of the legacies of coloni-
alism, and its dependence-orientated trading relationships are in part an
outgrowth of post-1945 reconstruction efforts. The present roles governing
the international trade were designed by the developed countries to suit the
needs of the developed countries. The developing countries have by and
large played the role of sideline spectators who occasionally get a piece of
the action, but only a small piece. But to be fair to the developed countries,
there has not been an active policy to 'keep the developing countries in their
places'. Instead the trading interests of the developing countries have simply
been overlooked as the developed countries pursued policies designed to
improve their individual positions.

The immediate post-war period was dominated by the idea that, to fight
international communism effectively, the Western economies must be rebuilt
at any cost. Since the United States emerged from the Second World War
largely intact, it was able to make a great contribution to reconstruction.
Economic-aid flows were tremendous but the bulk went to Europe and
Japan; little attention was paid to the economic problems of developing
countries.

As the reconstruction efforts proved successful, the industrial nations gradually implemented the rules of freer international trade, as embodied in the
Articles of the General Agreement on Tariffs and Trade (GATT). The trade
policies of the developed countries evolved along self-interest lines. Any
trade liberalisation introduced by one country was offered in return for a
concession gained from another; that is to say, tariff reductions were negotiated in GATT on the basis of reciprocity.

During this period the United States was the major supplier of badly
needed capital equipment. This lead to the so-called 'dollar scarcity'. In
order to earn additional dollars, the nations of Europe and Japan pursued
export-orientated trade policies. Consequently the GATT negotiations of

* Subsequently, Denmark, Ireland and the United Kingdom joined the E.E.C. From 1 January
1974 these participated in the preference scheme of the E.E.C. and, consequently, their individual schemes were terminated.
† The more developed socialist countries of Eastern Europe have also introduced preferential
trade measures in favour of the developing countries. However, because of a lack of information
on the operation and effects of these measures, preferences granted by the socialist countries will
not be covered in this book.

the day concentrated on market access. Those countries having the ability to pay for increased imports with dollars had the most influential positions in any GATT negotiations: thus the U.S. domination. Since the developing countries had no markets to speak of, and certainly no dollar resources, their trading interests were overlooked. In fact, for a number of reasons, the trade positions of the developing countries actually deteriorated during this period – if not in an absolute sense, certainly in a relative sense.

First, as is natural, these industrialised nations emphasised the rapidly growing markets for products which they could best produce, namely manufactures. Since the developing countries had little capacity to produce such products, the trade liberalisation which did occur, even though on a most-favoured-nation basis, was of little benefit to them.

Second, the nations of Europe became increasingly concerned about the economic domination of the United States. This is not to suggest serious conflicts among the allies, but that Europe wanted a bigger say in international economic (as well as political) matters. Recognising the limits of their individual influences, Europe evolved into two substantial trading blocs – the European Economic Community (E.E.C.) and the European Free Trade Area (EFTA). The elimination of tariff protection on intra-bloc trade placed exporters in countries outside the blocs at a disadvantage. In the short run the trade interests of the excluded developing countries suffered; but this does not mean that excluded countries will lose in the long run. It is very possible that, as a result of economic integration, the rate of economic growth of the bloc accelerated, thereby increasing the bloc's demand for imports. Such dynamic growth effects could therefore lead to a long-run stimulation of developing-country exports. However, in certain sectors, for reasons discussed below, this did not occur.

Third, the tremendous reconstruction which occurred after the Second World War was accompanied by serious structural problems inside the industrial nations. Economic incentives stimulated a large population movement from the farm to urban manufacturing centres. However, the skill levels of the labour force were not always compatible with the requirements of modern industry. The pressures of expanding international trade and technological innovation led to increasing pressures on governments to 'take care of the economically disadvantaged'. The result was increased protection against import competition for certain sectors of the economy. The agricultural policies of the day – based on price supports – dictated absolute protection against agricultural imports; and, increasingly, protectionist pressures came to bear on labour-intensive products, especially textiles and apparel. Thus, not only were the products of export interests to developing countries ignored in GATT tariff negotiations, but they also increasingly faced more restrictive trade barriers, such as quotas.

Fourth, the successive rounds of GATT tariff negotiations resulted in tariff structures in the developed countries which were decidedly biased against the trade interests of the developing countries. The typical profile of tariffs faced by developing-country exporters was that of a pyramid, i.e. zero or low duties on industrial raw materials, gradually escalating tariffs on non-traditional exports of semi-manufactured and manufactured products of higher-ordered processing, and very high duties on labour-intensive products whose international comparative advantage had shifted from the developed countries. This vertical ordering of tariffs acted as a further barrier to industrialisation by discouraging even the processing of locally available raw materials. For example, a developing country may export cocoa beans valued at $100 which are admitted, say, to the United States duty-free. If these cocoa beans were instead processed into cocoa butter, the export value might increase to $120; however, upon importation the United States might levy a 10 per cent tariff. Hence the creation of $20 of added value in the developing country by processing the beans into cocoa butter results in an increase in revenue of $20 less the $12 tariff charge, or only $8. It is highly possible that the resources used up in processing the beans into butter (i.e. processing costs) exceed $8, and hence the developing country is actually worse off as a result of processing its own raw materials into a higher-ordered good.

In addition to such policy initiatives taken by developed countries which ignore or actually injure the trade interests of developing countries, there are a number of natural forces which further erode the trade position of developing countries.[1] Among these are: (1) the slow rate of growth in world demand for products of export interest to the developing countries, primarily agricultural commodities and industrial raw materials; (2) the propensity of the industrial nations to develop synthetic substitutes for industrial commodities produced by developing countries; (3) the tendency for commodity prices to fluctuate, leading to uncertain export earnings; (4) the adverse relationship between export prices received by developing countries in comparison to prices paid for imports of capital equipment and other manufactures;* (5) the tendency for developing countries to experience perennial balance-of-payments deficits; (6) the fact that both world-wide recession and inflation result in a deterioration in the real value of developing-country export earnings; and so on. Though such problems are undoubtedly important, I will pay little attention to them in this book. The primary emphasis here is the role of preferential trading in redressing the existing international trading arrangements which evolved as a result of active policy initiatives and negotiations introduced primarily by the developed countries.

---

* This so-called 'declining terms of trade' argument has repeatedly been subjected to empirical investigation. The evidence to date denies its validity. Nevertheless, it has played an important political role in U.N. negotiations. More recently the emphasis has turned towards using commodity prices as a means of transferring more resources to developing countries via cartel pricing, such as in the example of petroleum.

THE FAILURE OF GATT

As briefly mentioned above, the existing rules governing international trade, as embodied in the Articles of GATT, were an outgrowth of the reconstruction efforts following the Second World War. Given the inter-war experience of world-wide depression, unacceptably high world unemployment, and the experience of competitive policies of unilateral protectionism, it is not surprising that the industrial nations desired some concept of law governing world trade. After all, the inter-war period of 'beggar-thy-neighbour' policies had contributed to the impoverishment of all trading partners. Looking at the post-war history from hindsight, we must conclude that the GATT experience is definitely preferable to the earlier experience. Nevertheless, the 'equitable' rules of GATT have not led to an 'equitable' benefit for all countries.

The crucial corner-stones of GATT are: (1) all nations should be treated equally in world-trade matters or that none should be discriminated against – the so-called 'most-favoured-nation' principle; and (2) when it is recognised that the rules governing trade are in need of revision, the new rules should provide for the mutual benefit of all concerned countries, i.e. revisions are to be negotiated on the basis of reciprocity. Such principles of non-discrimination and mutual benefit are difficult to disagree with; why is it that the developing countries are so disadvantaged under GATT?

First, equitable opportunities are truly equitable only among countries having equal trading abilities. But one should not expect countries having substantially different industrial structures to benefit equally. It should not be surprising that the industrially weaker developing countries have not fared particularly well under the non-discriminatory rules of GATT. Furthermore, as mentioned before, the application of the reciprocity principle has led to substantially reduced trade barriers on products of interest to the industrially strong nations, whereas products of interest to the developing countries have been ignored. This resulted because the developing countries had no explicit reciprocity to offer.*

The second reason is that there have been important exceptions to the rule, as the industrial nations have failed to comply with the rules and principles of GATT whenever such compliance would be injurious to their

---

* The industrial nations overlooked the real but unconventional reciprocity which the developing countries had to offer, namely any additional export earnings received by the developing countries as a result of a trade concession gained through GATT negotiations would be spent on imports from the industrial countries. Thus there is a one-to-one relationship between market access gained by the developing countries and hard-currency market access provided. And this implicit reciprocity does not require a reduction in developing-country trade barriers. Developing-country trade barriers affect their domestic industrial structures and product composition of imports, but not the aggregate level of imports. Thus any concession gained by the developing countries will be fully reciprocated by increased imports from the industrial nations.

domestic industries. A most notable example is the extreme protection afforded agricultural sectors by all industrial nations. Such protection is
terribly injurious to the export prospects of the developing countries. A
second and more revealing example is the case of textiles and apparel, which
have faced increasing degrees of protection as the developing countries have
increased their export capacity. In contrast to the agriculture example,
where protection has long existed, the textile example documents the tendency of the industrial nations to *increase* protection whenever the developing countries gain an international comparative advantage. A third example,
which was briefly touched upon earlier, is the tendency of the industrial
nations to violate the non-discrimination principle whenever it suits their
economic or political interests. The forerunners of such discrimination are
the colonial empires of the United Kingdom and France, discrimination
which was continued as their former colonies gained independence. These
agreements eventually led to the Commonwealth Preference Area, the
French Union, later to the E.E.C.–African Association agreements under the
Yaoundé Convention, and more recently to the enlarged European
Community's association with forty-six developing countries of Africa,
the Carribean and the Pacific under the Lomé Convention. The E.E.C. has
also negotiated a series of bilateral agreements with countries of the Mediterranean Basin. In addition to these discriminatory agreements between
the E.E.C. and numerous developing countries, the formation of the E.E.C.,
EFTA and the more recent free-trade area for Western Europe constitute
important introductions of discriminatory trading arrangements. A picture
is evolving of a West European-based trading bloc with the other nations of
the world left to fend for themselves. To the developing countries of Latin
America and Asia, access to European markets appears to be getting more
and more difficult in spite of GATT. And their alternative opportunities in
U.S. markets do not look all that bright in light of the recent protectionist
tendencies in that country.

It should be recognised, however, that the GATT forum has increasingly
taken note of the trade problems of the developing countries. The 'Haberler
Report', sponsored by GATT, documented a GATT recognition that
industrial-country trade barriers played an important role in retarding the
rate of growth of developing-country exports.[2] As a consequence, the problem of expanding developing-country exports was placed on the GATT
agenda. Resulting negotiations led to the 1961 Declaration on Promotion of
the Trade of Less Developed Countries and eventually to the 1963 Programme of Action. The Programme of Action contained a host of elements
including: (1) a standstill on new tariff and non-tariff barriers to trade for
products of export interest to developing countries; (2) the elimination of
quantitative restrictions on imports from developing countries by 31
December 1965 at the latest; (3) duty-free entry for tropical products; and (4)
the reduction and elimination of tariffs on developing-country exports of

semi-processed products (presumably including semi-processed agricultural items).

The major indictment of GATT is that little of substance has resulted from the Programme of Action. In fact, the renewed GATT Arrangement Regarding International Trade in Textiles, calling for 'voluntary export restrictions' for textile and apparel trade, represents a change in the opposite direction from the 'standstill' principle. It is this inaction in GATT that has contributed to the developing countries' de-emphasis on GATT initiatives and instead has led them to concentrate on the more sympathetic forum of the United Nations.

TRADE AND DEVELOPMENT IN THE UNITED NATIONS

By the mid-1950s the developing countries were gaining sufficient influence in the United Nations to stimulate discussions on issues of trade and development. Their numbers were gradually increasing as more and more dependent colonies became independent nations. Thus there occurred a gradual shift in U.N. emphasis towards economic and social questions.

By 1961 at the Sixteenth Session of the U.N. General Assembly, the developing countries introduced a resolution calling for a conference on international trade and development. The vote was forty-five for, thirty-six against with ten abstentions; the primary opposition was by the rich countries of the West. After additional pressure, it was finally agreed that such a conference should be held (Resolution 917(XXXIV) of the U.N. Economic and Social Council (ECOSOC), 3 August 1962). At the urging of the United States, Japan and Uruguay, the U.N. Secretary-General appointed a Group of Experts to identify the trade problems of the developing countries, in order to assess the activities of related international organisations and to find overlaps and voids. Many felt this was simply a delaying tactic, but in any event the conference was now on the international agenda, scheduled to be convened not later than 1964.

During 1963–4 a Preparatory Committee met to agree on an agenda, to make the administrative arrangements and to supervise the preparation of appropriate background documentation. Dr Raul Prebisch was appointed Secretary-General of the conference to lead the Preparatory Committee. Two major documents emerged. The first was a report by the Group of Experts – *Commodity and Trade Problems of Developing Countries: Institutional Arrangements* – which presented two opposing views for reform: (1) to reform the existing international institutional arrangements, i.e. improve the use of GATT; and (2) to create a new independent agency to negotiate matters of trade and development. In between these extremes was the alternative which eventually emerged, the creation of a permanent organ within the United Nations.

The second major document was the report of the Secretary-General –

Towards a New Trade Policy for Development – the so-called 'Prebisch Report'. This report, as evidenced by hindsight, previewed the decisions taken at UNCTAD I (though not necessarily implemented) and set the stage for organising the activities of the UNCTAD Secretariat, an organisational structure which is amazingly intact even today, some twelve years later.

The conference met in 1964 and proved to be little more than a confrontation between the rich countries of the West and the developing countries, which were generally supported by the socialist countries of Eastern Europe. The end result was a 'wish list' emphasising the desires of the developing countries – economic growth rather than stability and a call for the international community to recognise and take into account the differences in the levels of economic development among countries. In essence, the developing countries wanted to be developed, but since they could not accomplish this alone, they wanted help on a preferential basis.

By far the most important outcome of the conference had nothing to do with substantive economic trade and development issues: instead it was the unity of purpose demonstrated by the developing countries' recognition that their individual impotence in international negotiations could be offset by co-ordinated action, i.e. presenting a united front. The importance of the emergence of the Group of 77,* a united group of developing countries voting as a block in favour of positions which they had earlier arrived at through internal compromise, cannot be overestimated. The second major outcome of the conference was the establishment of UNCTAD as a permanent U.N. Secretariat. Some observers would contend that the order of importance be reversed, but the two are probably so interdependent that the answer to this question is immaterial.

However, this developing-country unity presented as many new problems as it solved. In the first place, unity among the developing countries is much more difficult to achieve than unity among the rich. Since the thrust of the initiatives presented to UNCTAD is for the rich countries to grant one kind of concession or another – all of which come at a cost to the rich – the developed countries can generally agree to oppose most initiatives. On the other hand, the developing countries have very little in common other than their relative poverty. Almost any *specific* trade-related initiative will benefit at most only a few developing countries. Thus, in order to reach a position which all or most of the developing countries can support from a self-benefit point of view, the concessions requested must be quite broad and all-encompassing. This problem has led to developing-country *demands* for concessions, variously described as 'wish lists' or 'shooting for the moon' –

---

* Developing-country unity did not actually originate in UNCTAD I. At the 1963 session of the U.N. General Assembly a Joint Declaration of the Developing Countries was signed by seventy-five countries. By 1976, when UNCTAD IV was held, membership in the now permanently named Group of 77 had grown to 111 developing countries.

i.e. concessions that are far beyond anything which the developed countries are willing or even able to give.

This problem leads directly to a second one, namely, with their large voting majority, the developing countries could, in principle, vote themselves anything they wished. However, they recognise that the UNCTAD forum has no enforcement powers. If the developing countries vote themselves something that the developed world is unwilling to grant, the relevant UNCTAD resolution would not be implemented.

A few of the more militant developing countries feel that their voting majority should be used often to emphasise the differences between the rich and poor countries. Others, however, feel that voting along such group lines would simply highlight a failure in the negotiation process. They realise that one major value of the UNCTAD forum is that it serves to publicise developing-country problems, thereby raising sympathetic and humanitarian emotions among the peoples of the developed world. Such a world press campaign will be most effective if the developing countries appear willing to compromise during the negotiations.

This desire to compromise has led to a negotiation process which is somewhat unique to UNCTAD, the so-called 'group system'. The members of UNCTAD are divided into four groups – Group A contains developing countries in Africa, Asia and Yugoslavia; Group B the O.E.C.D. countries; Group C Latin American countries; and Group D the socialist countries of Eastern Europe. Before each negotiation session the groups meet separately to decide on a common position. At the formal sessions, the group positions are argued by choosen spokesmen. Of course individual delegates can also raise issues of special concern to their own countries, but generally individuals do not speak against the over-all position of their group.

The prospects for compromise is further enhanced by a rather unique conciliation process developed by UNCTAD. Decisions taken by the Conference require a two-thirds majority.* However, before acting on any decision which involves the economic or financial interest of any country, a request for conciliation may be submitted.† When a request is submitted voting is suspended and the issue is referred to a small *ad hoc* body – called a 'contact group' – composed of interested parties, based on an equitable geographical distribution. The contact group does not vote; instead it re-

---

* The conference meets every four years. Between conferences, the day-to-day affairs are handled by a standing committee – the Trade and Development Board consisting of fifty-five members elected by the conference on a regional allocation basis (twenty-two from Group A, eighteen from Group B, nine from Group C and six from Group D). Decisions of the board are made by simple majority. The board is empowered to establish other committees, including the Committees on Commodities (fifty-five members), Manufactures, Invisibles, Finance and Shipping (forty-five members each).

† This procedure is quasi-automatic as it can be started by a small number of countries – ten for a conference, five for the board and three for any committee.

ports to the next session of the conference, board or committee, as the case may be. Depending on the outcome of the conciliation process, the subsequent vote may adopt (or refuse) the issue (usually stated in the form of a resolution) unanimously or by majority vote. By far the majority of decisions taken by UNCTAD come out of the conciliation process in a form which is adopted by unanimous concent. Generally, whenever a formal vote is taken on a particular issue it means that the compromise procedure has broken down and that no mutually acceptable position could be found; the vote simply documents the frustrations.

One can probably say that this conciliation process forms a major cornerstone of UNCTAD since all serious negotiations take place in these contact groups. It is here that the developing country 'wish list' is pared down to something which the developed countries can accept. Unfortunately, the end result is often a compromise resolution phrased in generalities supporting the moral position of the developing countries while containing sufficient 'loop-holes' for the developed countries so that the concessions negotiated often contain only minor economic advantages for the developing countries.

POLITICAL ISSUES SURROUNDING PREFERENCES

To tell the story of all the political plots and counter-plots surrounding the G.S.P. would require a multi-volume effort.[3] My purpose here is the more modest objective of highlighting some of the major political influences which played a role in shaping the provisions of the preference system.[4] The three major groups of countries – developing, socialist and developed (O.E.C.D.) – had competing interests. The developing countries desired increased access to O.E.C.D.-country markets. The socialist countries wished goodwill from the developing countries and a chance to highlight the evils of the developed countries of the West. The O.E.C.D. countries played a defensive game attempting to safeguard the *status quo* while appearing to be sympathetic to the trade and development problems facing the developing countries. If economic power were left to dictate the outcome (the *status quo*), only the socialist countries of Eastern Europe would emerge victorious.

This left the O.E.C.D. countries with quite a dilemma. To give in on the economic issues would cause serious domestic political conflicts as improved access to their markets would cause charges of import injury to domestic producers.* In addition, the preferential nature of the proposed

---

* At any time various groups of domestic workers and firms are facing economic difficulties which are attributed to unfair import competition. Closer examination reveals that, in the vast majority of such cases, the real difficulties are due to either a declining domestic market or to the inability of the particular group to effectively compete with other domestic producers. Nevertheless, the import-competition scapegoat is offered (sometimes under the argument that reduced imports would enlarge the market potential for the less efficient domestic producers). Numerous examples are provided in the reports of the U.S. Tariff Commission (renamed the

changes in market access favouring developing-country exports would also harm export prospects in other preference-giving-country markets. Thus, O.E.C.D. governments had to contend with anti-G.S.P. pressures from both the import-competing protectionist lobbies and the export-orientated trade-expansion lobbies. In this case the governments were not asked to walk the normal tightrope between protectionism and trade expansion; instead they were asked to walk up the face of a waterfall, meeting all the political pressures head-on. Their only serious support came from the foreign-policy groups, who saw the importance of improving political relations with the Third World as an important step in countering the many threats to peace in the world.

At the 1964 UNCTAD Conference, the economic forces prevailed and no agreement was reached favouring a G.S.P. The United States was the primary opponent, arguing that the small potential for exporting manufactured products by developing countries would generate insufficient benefit to justify upsetting the corner-stone principal of GATT – non-discrimination. Also, M.F.N. rates on such products would be so low after the Kennedy Round that the preferential tariff margins created by a G.S.P. would be too small to significantly stimulate developing-country exports. Such meagre benefits could not justify creating developing-country vested interests against future tariff reductions. Finally, setting a precedent of discriminatory trading might lead to other discriminatory practices, including the regionalisation of world trade along inefficient lines of production. Such reservations were also held by Canada, Japan, Switzerland – and to a lesser extent by Norway and Sweden.

The problem of E.E.C. support was more the result of internal disagreement than opposition to the principle of preferential trading. West Germany and the Netherlands favoured a single generalised preferential scheme for all developed countries – to be introduced by all industrialised countries. Belgium and France, on the other hand, wanted selective preferences to be negotiated bilaterally between an industrial country (or group) and a developing country (or group). Such a system was aimed at preserving the trading interests of the associated African states; this approach would enable each developed country to use preferences to promote its own economic and political ends.

The importance of the African states associated with the E.E.C. in creating the G.S.P. is much greater than their importance in using it will ever be. They increasingly urged France and the European Commission to provide a favourable voice in the UNCTAD discussions, to press the United States for her consent. Their objective was to obtain preferential access in U.S. markets. But at the same time they were very concerned about their own special access to European markets; the E.E.C. was urged to take their trading

International Trade Commission by the Trade Act of 1974) on investigations pursuant to applications of escape-clause action or import-relief measures.

interests into account when designing the E.E.C. scheme of preferences (and thus the French–Belgium position favouring 'selective preferences').

Their strategy played a significant role in accomplishing a part of their objective – U.S. agreement to participate in the G.S.P. However, the results of U.S. participation were not exactly as anticipated. The U.S. submission to international political pressure was entirely defensive; in no way does it reflect a change of heart or a new-found belief that the G.S.P. would generate meaningful trade benefits for the developing countries. Instead the United States was looking at events in Europe, and especially the regionalisation of world trade, brought about by the Yaoundé Convention between the E.E.C. and the African Associates, thus providing for two-way preferential trading arrangements. Such arrangements discriminated against U.S. exports to Africa and, not incidentally, discriminated against Latin American exports to Europe.* In fact, the U.S. formal announcement in favour of the G.S.P. came at the 14 April 1967 Punta del Este meeting of the American Chiefs of State in order to maximise the effect on Latin America. Even though the United States was making political hay in Latin America, it was really attempting to stop the regionalisation of world trade in Afro-Europe as well as in America.† The United States came to favour non-discriminatory preferences for all developing countries as more desirable than a regionalisation of world trade based on selective preferences. U.S. opposition to regionalisation was so strong that at the 1968 New Delhi meeting of UNCTAD, the U.S. agreement in principle to the concept of generalised preferences was accompanied by the promise that any developing country which participated in a preferential trade agreement (i.e. granted preferential access to non-U.S. exports or received preferential access in any industrial-country market) would be denied preferential access under the U.S. G.S.P.‡ Thus, the U.S. submission to the G.S.P. was an attempt to generate developing-country opposition to the E.E.C. policy of regionalising world trade through preferential trading arrangements (see Chapter 8).

Once the United States agreed in principle to consider seriously the introduction of preferential tariffs in favour of developing-country exports, negotiations towards that end proceeded quite rapidly. The developed countries of the West (O.E.C.D.) met in Paris to decide among themselves what the preference system should look like. At the 1968 New Delhi meeting of

---

* At this time the United States was not too concerned about any inability of U.S. exports to compete with African exports in E.E.C. markets. However, when the E.E.C. expanded its policy to include preferential arrangements with Mediterranean countries, U.S. exports of certain agricultural products, such as citrus fruits and juices, became a concern.

† This U.S. submission came on the heels of an Inter-American Committee on the Alliance for Progress recommendation for vertical preferences in the United States as defensive measures against the Afro-European bloc whereby some developing countries enjoy preferences outside of the American hemisphere plus non-discriminatory access to U.S. markets.

‡ This position was later relaxed to allow developing countries to enjoy preferential access to industrial-country markets without loss of U.S. G.S.P. treatment (see Chapter 3).

UNCTAD a unanimous agreement was reached that a generalised system of preferences should be established – though substantial disagreement between developed and developing countries still remained concerning particular provisions. At the 1970 meeting of the UNCTAD Special Committee on Preferences, these differences were sufficiently resolved to go ahead with the implementation of formal preferential tariff schemes.

Only one problem remained. The G.S.P., built upon the principle of preferential (i.e. discriminatory) treatment, violated the first Article of GATT – the most-favoured-nation principle. Before the G.S.P. could be implemented, the contracting parties of GATT would have to exempt trade under the G.S.P. provisions from the M.F.N. principle. The legal authorisation came in June 1971 when a ten-year waiver to the M.F.N. principle of Article I was voted by the contracting parties; and the way was cleared for the introduction of the first G.S.P. scheme by the E.E.C. on 1 July 1971.

2

Economic Impact of Tariff Preferences

The immediate objective of tariff preferences in favour of the developing countries is to expand their exports and export earnings. This objective is to be accomplished through static price advantages making developing-country exports of manufactured products more competitive *vis-à-vis* both domestic production and imports from third countries; such a price advantage is hoped to bring with it the more important dynamic incentives for new investment in export capacity. The ultimate objective is of course to stimulate economic development through industrialisation.

The emphasis on industrialisation is understandable even in light of the recent international food crisis. There are limited opportunities to increase both employment and labour productivity in either the agricultural or the extractive sectors. As evidenced by the historical experience of the industrial nations of the West, increased productivity in the agricultural sectors results in more and more workers being released and therefore dependent upon other sectors for employment opportunities. Industrialisation is necessary to absorb these redundant workers. Furthermore, industrialisation provides ample opportunities for increasing labour productivity through technological innovation – rising labour productivity being a crucial precondition for long-term increases in living standards.

Before examining the likely effectiveness of tariff preferences as a policy tool for stimulating industrialisation, it seems appropriate to ask: Why did the developing countries resort to a strategy involving several years of international negotiations with the ultimate decision resting with the developed countries? Could not the developing countries have created the same export-orientated price advantages through alternative domestic policy initiatives? In international trade matters, such a question is almost always answered in the affirmative. This particular case is no exception.

The most obvious export-stimulating measure that any country can take is to devalue its currency. Such a move would fail only when trading partners resort to retaliatory devaluations of their own. However, it is unlikely that the group of developed countries of the West would risk upsetting their structure of exchange rates simply to retaliate against individual developing-country devaluations especially when the developing countries account for such a small share of world trade. In any case it would be much easier for the developing countries to negotiate even extreme joint currency devaluations than it was to negotiate tariff preferences. Why not the devaluation policy?

The problem with devaluation is that the market exchange rate for a currency determines not only what you receive for exports of a particular product, but it also determines what you receive for other products. Many of the developing countries rely heavily on exports of agricultural commodities and/or industrial raw materials for the bulk of their export earnings. Such products have quite low price elasticities, implying that devaluation would reduce the export earnings derived from such products. It is unlikely that the increased earnings from exports of manufactured products (even when they have relatively high elasticities) would be sufficient to offset the loss in earnings from traditional commodity exports. To put it another way, the exchange rate appropriate for stimulating exports of non-traditional manufactured products is generally lower than that needed to maximise the foreign-exchange earnings from exporting agricultural commodities and industrial raw materials. In this case, the developing country faces a dilemma: Do you maximise current foreign-exchange earnings by maintaining a high exchange rate or do you stimulate the exportation of manufactures for industrialisation to be achieved over the longer run by maintaining a low exchange rate?

However, this dilemma can be solved by combining exchange-rate policy with an appropriate export tax/subsidy programme. If the exportation of manufactures is stimulated by devaluation, traditional export earnings can be maintained by imposing export taxes on agricultural commodities and industrial raw materials. Alternatively, if export earnings are protected by maintaining a high exchange rate, manufacturing stimulation can be accomplished by subsidising such exports.* The only problem is that in both of these cases the developing country is faced with financing the export-expansion policy – either by direct subsidy or by reducing the foreign exchange price of exports via devaluation. On the other hand, if the exportation of manufactured products is stimulated by tariff preferences, the financing burden is borne by citizens of the importing developed country.† In this case developing-country export earnings from traditional products are maintained while exports and export earnings from manufactured products are stimulated.

---

* This policy is less attractive than the former since its effectiveness depends on the non-administration of anti-dumping or anti-export subsidy policies, e.g. the U.S. countervailing-duty laws.

† This is a slight simplification. From a welfare point of view the 'net burden' to the importing country may be negative if the increased consumer surplus exceeds the loss of producer surplus plus the decline in tariff revenue. In all likelihood this will be the case, especially since preferential tariff reductions tend to protect domestic producers at the expense of third-country exporters. To be correct, the burden is financed by the importing-country government (in forgone tariff revenues), by export-competing producers in third countries, and by import-competing producers in the importing country; importing-country consumers receive a benefit in the form of lower-priced imported goods.

But the rationale for tariff preferences cannot rest entirely on its contribution to *financing* the stimulus to increased exports. Traditionally, the developed countries have been willing to provide financing through direct aid; if an increase in financial resources is all that is being sought, negotiations for increased aid would be more fruitful than negotiations to revise international trading rules. The developed countries would certainly be more willing to concede increased aid flows than to consent to opening the door for overt trade discrimination by agreeing to an international trade policy which is contrary to the corner-stone principle of GATT – the most-favoured-nation principle.

The financial demands of industrialisation are obvious. The machinery and technology necessary for efficient production are most often not available in developing countries; therefore they must be imported. Similarly the complementary infrastructure must be built at no small cost. But in addition industrialisation typically requires mass-market outlets for the manufactured products in order for an efficient scale of operation to be reached. Most developing countries have an insufficient population to provide a feasible domestic market for manufactured products; and even in the larger developing countries, the share of the population which can reasonably be considered to be participating in the local market economy is often too small to justify optimum plant scales. Thus a very crucial prerequisite to efficient industrial production cannot be provided domestically even if additional financial flows from abroad were available – an international trade policy is necessary.

The tariff-preferences policy, therefore, is a logical extension of the 'infant-industry' argument for temporary protection. The growth from infancy requires a protected market which is large enough to justify efficient production – such a market is not available at home. It can only be provided by protecting world markets for developing-country exports of manufactured products.

The need for protected markets derives from the fact that in developing countries the low wages are generally accompanied by even lower labour productivity. Even when the wage/productivity trade-off yields lower processing costs, total costs in developing countries are still too high due to such factors as the high costs of input materials and components, high transport costs to world markets, high quality-control rejection rates, high costs of replacement parts and other elements in maintaining capital equipment, excessive power interruptions and plant shut-downs, and so on. In the main, developing-country producers are unable to compete with producers in the industrial nations under most-favoured-nation conditions. A competitive advantage is needed which, they hope, will be provided by the system of preferential tariffs favouring developing-country exports of manufactured and semi-manufactured products.

BENEFITS FOR DEVELOPING COUNTRIES

Preferential trading arrangements have traditionally been analysed in terms of trade creation and trade diversion, with the ultimate aim of determining whether world welfare increases or decreases. Welfare increases to the extent that imports from a preferred source displace less efficient domestic production; and welfare decreases to the extent that imports from a preferred source displace more efficiently produced imports from a non-preferred source.

Trade creation is beneficial to world welfare because the resource cost of producing the related imports is reduced; the released resources in the importing country can then be used to produce alternative goods and services. Of course the value of the released resources overstates the welfare gain since resources are required by the preferred country to produce the goods exported; the resource saving could be measured as the difference in the resource requirements to produce a unit of the particular product. In addition to the resource saving there is a benefit to consumers – who are now able to consume a larger quantity at a lower price. Since both of these components (resource saving and consumer benefit) are positive, the over-all effect of trade creation is to improve world welfare.*

The effect of trade diversion is less clear. Whenever the preferential tariff is large enough to cause importers to switch their source of supply from more efficient non-preferred sources to less efficient preferred sources, the resource cost of imports will increase. World welfare decreases by the net resource wastage. However, as in the case of trade creation, consumers in the importing country benefit because of the larger volume of lower-priced imports, and the nation loses to the extent of the decline in tariff revenue. Thus the over-all effect of trade diversion on world welfare is uncertain.

The total impact of preferential trading arrangements, which both liberalises and distorts world trade, depends upon the relative magnitudes of trade creation and trade diversion. A large trade creation is most likely when the preferred countries and the importing (preference-giving) country have similar economic structures, thereby increasing the opportunity for a tariff preference to result in preferred imports displacing domestic production. If the economic structures are quite different, the scope for trade creation is significantly reduced. Likewise the prospects for a large trade-diversion element are enhanced if the economic structures of preferred countries and non-preferred countries are similar.

---

* For the importing country alone, the welfare effect comprises a decline in producer surplus, a loss of tariff revenue and an increase in consumer surplus. If the developing countries as a group have a highly elastic export supply function for manufactures, the importing-country consumer-surplus gain will more than offset the decline in producer surplus and the loss in tariff revenue.

In the case of tariff preferences for developing countries which have been introduced by industrial countries, the economic structures of the preferred countries and the preference-giving countries are dissimilar, thus indicating that trade creation is likely to be quite small; but at the same time the major non-preferred suppliers are by and large these same industrial countries. That is to say, the non-preferred sources for the U.S. preference system are the E.E.C., Japan, Canada and the other preference-giving countries; similarly the non-preferred sources for the E.E.C. preference system are the United States, Japan, non-E.E.C. West European countries, and so on. Thus the economic structures of the preferred and non-preferred countries also differ, thereby minimising the magnitude of trade diversion.

In conclusion, the impact of tariff preferences favouring the developing countries on world welfare, as traditionally measured by the concepts of trade creation and trade diversion, is likely to be negligibly small.[1] But this conclusion should not be taken to mean that tariff preferences have little value. Even if world welfare remains unchanged, the redistribution of world income in favour of developing countries might increase the welfare value of a constant (or even declining) level of world income.[2] Furthermore, welfare measurements based on the concepts of trade creation and trade diversion assume that factors of production have alternative employment opportunities (i.e. welfare is measured in terms of consumer and producer surplus). But in developing countries it is probable that some of the increased exports generate employment of otherwise unemployed or underemployed resources. In such cases the contribution to welfare is the entire factor wage bill, not just the producer surplus. On the other hand, resources displaced in the preference-giving importing countries, as well as resources displaced in the non-preferred exporting countries (i.e. other developed countries), are likely to be re-employed; to the extent permanent unemployment results, world welfare will be reduced.* When such factors as income redistribution and changes in the level of employment are incorporated into the welfare calculations, the result will in all likelihood show a noticeable increase in world welfare.

The above considerations have been primarily based on static adjustments. But as is well known in international trade theory, the major benefits to be derived from the formation of customs unions, free-trade areas and other preferential trading arrangements result from what are called 'dynamic' factors – i.e. shifts in demand and supply functions. In fact, the entire argument for 'infant-industry' protection is premised on the belief that a non-competitive industry will become competitive due to gradual improvements in production efficiency. It is true that the dynamic factors normally considered in the formation of a customs union or free-trade area are some-

---

* World welfare must also be reduced by the value of resources required to re-allocate those resources that are displaced and which then become re-employed.

what different than those likely to result from tariff preferences. Normally the enlargement of the 'domestic' market facilitates more efficient economies of scale in production. Increased productivity leads to increased income, further increasing market size, investment, and so on. The end result is a faster rate of economic growth. On the other hand, since tariff preferences are a one-way street, such dynamic benefits will not directly accrue to the preference-giving industrial countries. Instead the major impact will fall on the preference-receiving developing countries through improved access to world markets, opportunities for larger-scale production, increased exports and income, enlarged domestic markets for domestic production, and so on.

In addition we might observe new export flows of non-traditional products from the preference beneficiaries, products which were previously non-competitive in world markets and thereby limited to local developing-country markets. Such products may have initially been imported by developing countries and later produced there behind an import-substitution wall or other barrier to trade. Finally, the more indirect dynamic factors should not be overlooked: factors such as the tariff-margin incentives for investment in new export capacity by local firms and multinational corporations; importers in developed countries searching for sources of supply in developing countries for products previously imported from other developed countries as well as for new import products; and developing-country suppliers establishing new marketing linkages in the preference-giving countries. Such indirect incentives are almost impossible to quantify as they become evident only over rather long time periods. Nevertheless, they may very well be the most important considerations for evaluating the impact of tariff preferences.

IMPORTANCE OF TARIFFS AS A BARRIER TO TRADE

One of the major arguments against tariff preferences was that after the Kennedy Round of tariff negotiations the average level of duties imposed by the developed countries on manufactured imports would be so low that even their complete elimination on a preferential basis would provide only an inconsequential stimulus for developing-country exports. After all, the post-Kennedy Round tariffs of the O.E.C.D. countries averaged 10 per cent or less. Such a small tariff margin would be more than eaten up by the excessive transport costs, productive inefficiencies in the developing countries, the additional costs associated with importing crucial input materials and components (or purchasing such materials from inefficient domestic producers who are producing behind an import-substitution tariff wall), and so on. Just how important are tariffs as a barrier to developing-country exports?

This point served as the basis for the U.S. argument against tariff preferences throughout the pre-1968 period of UNCTAD negotiations. This view was further supported when the developing countries' exports were examined more closely, product by product. The bulk of developing-country exports involved products which either faced very low duties (e.g. tropical agricultural commodities and industrial raw materials) or faced rigid barriers of trade of a non-tariff nature (e.g. some agricultural commodities and textiles). Tariff preferences would not affect the latter group of products and could hardly stimulate trade in the former group.

This position was effectively rebutted by the UNCTAD Secretariat in a careful examination of the tariff structures of the developed countries.[3] It was shown that the level of tariff protection against imports rises with the level of processing. Such a tariff structure discourages the processing of raw materials and instead encourages their exportation in raw form.* It is therefore not surprising that the existing structure of developing-country exports is heavily biased against manufactures and in favour of exporting materials in a crude state. The developing countries argue that the existing structure of their exports is in part a logical outgrowth of the incentives (and disincentives) embodied in the developed-country tariff structures. Further, changing these incentives can be expected to change the future structure of developing-country exports.

This point has been more forcefully demonstrated by introducing the concept of 'effective protection'.[4] In essence, tariff protection enables domestic producers to be less efficient (i.e. to incur higher costs) than their foreign competitors; the extent of permissible domestic inefficiency is limited by the height of the tariff.† If input materials and components are available to all producers (domestic and foreign) at world prices, the entire degree of inefficiency provided to domestic producers by the tariff can occur in the domestic processing activity (domestic value-added). This means that, for example, when half of the value of a product is accounted for by processing (the other half accounted for by materials and components purchased by the producer), a nominal tariff of, say, 10 per cent enables the domestic producer to be 20 per cent less efficient than his foreign competitor.‡ And this ignores a number of additional costs borne by foreign producers but not by domestic producers – such costs as international transportation (15 per cent of the value of the shipment), legal and other import documentation costs (10

---

* As pointed out in Chapter 1, such a tariff structure severely penalises developing-country processing and could very well reduce the export earnings to be derived from processing activities to a level smaller than the processing resource costs.

† This of course ignores transport costs and other trading costs not associated with domestic production and marketing. The tariff simply provides an additional degree of permissible inefficiency.

‡ This example is quite representative for a wide range of finished manufactured goods which typically are made using input materials and components which account for 40–50 per cent of the total costs of production. The nominal tariff rate of 10 per cent is simply the approximate average of the post-Kennedy Round M.F.N. tariff rates applicable to industrial-country imports of manufactured goods.

per cent), and so on.[5] If these factors are incorporated into our comparison, the domestic producer will remain competitive even if his processing costs exceed those of the foreign exporter by as much as 45 per cent. Of course this example is simply representative and illustrative; the actual effective protection provided by the tariff rate which applies to a specific product depends on the actual share of total costs accounted for by domestic processing; and of course such shares differ from product to product. But the types of processing which take place in developing countries often involve simple assembly operations, sewing of textiles, transforming local raw materials into lower-ordered semi-manufactures, and the like; each of these activities contributes little to the final value of the goods. In the case of processing cocoa beans into cocoa butter (our example from Chapter 1), the processing added only 20 per cent to the value of the raw material (that is, domestic processing accounts for $16\frac{2}{3}$ per cent of the total value); in this case a 10 per cent tariff enables the developed-country processor of cocoa beans to be a full 60 per cent less efficient than a developing-country processor. Upon adding transport costs and other import costs, the 'effective protection' afforded the developed-country processor climbs to roughly 85 per cent.

The above must be adjusted to the extent that domestic producers must pay duties on importable materials and components; such duties penalise local producers whenever their foreign competitors have duty-free access to these input materials. Normally, however, developing-country producers gain very little from this element since developed countries grant duty-free entry (or have very low duties) on almost all industrial raw materials. And for assembly operations, the sources of supply for the components are the developed countries themselves. In this area the trade policies of the developing countries are more important, putting their own exporters at a competitive disadvantage. For many standardised, non-technical materials and components, rather inefficient developing-country producers are protected in their local markets by import-substitution trade barriers. Consequently, developing-country exporters are often forced to incur excessive input costs, thereby increasing the competitive advantage possessed by local producers in developed countries.[6]

The main point to be derived from the above discussion is that, given the relatively low nominal rate of duty, tariffs imposed by developed countries on imports from developing countries are likely to be a much greater hindrance to trade than one would expect. It is not so much the level of tariff that is important but rather the structure of tariffs, the extent to which processing activities involve purchases of input materials and components, and the extent to which producers (domestic as well as foreign) have access to inputs at world (or tariff-ridden) prices. Given the steeply escalated tariff structures of the developed countries, the high dependence of developing-country producers on imported materials and components and the import-substitution policies of the developing countries, we must conclude that tariffs do provide a significant barrier to developing-country exports of manufactured and semi-manufactured products.

The advantages which developing-country exports might gain as a result of preferential tariff reductions fall into two categories: (1) the reduction in protection afforded domestic producers in the preference-giving country; and (2) a competitive edge gained *vis-à-vis* competing exports in non-preferred countries.

Under the preferential tariff system, duty-free access is provided for a very broad range of manufactured and semi-manufactured products. This completely eliminates the escalation properties of developed-country tariff structures. Thus developing-country exporters no longer face the above-mentioned disincentives to process their own raw materials or to assemble developed-country components. The protection of domestic producers is completely eliminated *vis-à-vis* developing-country exporters. In fact, the resulting tariff system may provide the developing-country suppliers with a competitive advantage even over domestic suppliers. Since M.F.N. duties still apply for trade among developed countries, preference-giving-country suppliers must pay duties on imported materials and components which originate in other developed countries. Thus domestic producers face an 'implicit' tax on processing which creates so-called 'negative effective protection'. If developing-country suppliers have access to these same materials and components free of duty (or if the developing country has a policy to kick-back input duties on exported products), they will gain a competitive advantage *vis-à-vis* these preference-giving-country suppliers. The reduction in effective protection will be in the order of 20 per cent for the United States and the E.E.C., 12 per cent for Sweden and 30 per cent for Japan.[7] On the other hand, developing-country import-substitution policies which protect an inefficient materials-producing industry will eliminate this latter advantage for their exporters; however, the effective protection facing their exports will still be reduced to zero by the preferential tariff system.

Similarly, developing-country exports will gain a competitive advantage over non-preferred exports which is greater than that indicated by the rate of duty alone. The same effective-protection concepts operate in that the entire price advantage can be applied to the local processing activities. Since this advantage is not offset by preference-giving-country duties being imposed on non-preferred-country materials and components, the magnitude of the competitive advantage *vis-à-vis* non-preferred exporters is greater than *vis-à-vis* domestic producers. This preferential advantage has been estimated by Professor H. G. Johnson for a number of manufacturing industries covering intermediate products, consumer goods and investment goods; the averages for his estimates are 46 per cent for the United States, 37 per cent for the E.E.C., 26 per cent for Sweden and 53 per cent for Japan.[8] In addition, the 'implicit' tax on non-preferred-country processing also operates whenever the country imposes M.F.N. duties on importable inputs (provided the developing-country suppliers have access to such materials and components at world prices or under duty kick-back provisions).

In summary, the importance of tariff preferences on the competitive position of developing-country *processing activities* in world markets is likely to be much greater than one would anticipate given the level of preferential margins implicit in existing M.F.N. tariffs. But the economic impact of this new system depends upon other factors as well – such factors as import-substitution policies of developing countries, the structure of world transport costs, the effectiveness of developing-country export-market and distribution channels, their productive efficiencies and quality control, and so on.

Of equal importance is an element which has been overlooked completely up to this point, namely the rules and regulations instituted by the preference-giving countries to govern preferential trading. It is very unlikely that the preference-giving countries are simply going to open their doors to imports from developing countries; instead they are likely to take precautions to safeguard domestic producers. In so doing they might exclude certain manufactured products from preferential treatment; they might impose limits on the volume of preference-receiving trade; they might provide for escape-clause-type relief in those cases where developing-country exports threaten injury to domestic producers; and so on. In addition, they might introduce measures to guarantee that all developing countries share to some extent in the benefits; such measures might take the form of limitations for the more competitive developing countries. In Part 2 these rules and regulations are described and analysed to determine their likely impact on international trade under the preferential tariff system.

PART 2

Operation of the System of Tariff Preferences

Introduction to Part 2

In negotiating the G.S.P., the preference-giving countries initially hoped to agree on a common system benefiting a common list of developing countries. However, because of differing social, economic and political pressures among them, no such common system was possible; instead each so-called 'donor' introduced its own unique preference scheme. Thus the G.S.P. consists of eleven different schemes (ignoring the preferential arrangements introduced by the developed socialist countries of Eastern Europe), each scheme identifying the developing countries which would benefit, the products which would qualify for preferential treatment, and the rules and regulations which would apply.

Part 2 examines the operation and effects of the G.S.P., taking into consideration the precise institutional features of each preference scheme. The economic and political issues surrounding the designation of beneficiary developing countries are described in Chapter 3. Chapter 4 identifies the precise lists of products to be covered by the G.S.P., more importantly those products to be excluded from preferential treatment because of a fear of excessive import competition from developing-country exports. The special measures introduced to safeguard domestic producers in the donor countries from unanticipated injurious import competition are covered in Chapter 5. Chapter 6 describes the rules which were introduced to guarantee that goods imported under G.S.P. tariff treatment are actually produced in a beneficiary developing country rather than simply being transhipped through 'trading houses'. Finally, Chapter 7 evaluates the operation of the G.S.P., presenting estimates of the trade benefits accruing to the developing countries as well as estimates of the production and employment costs borne by the donor countries. The major conclusions drawn from this evaluation are as follows: first, that the trade benefits of the G.S.P. are quite meagre; second, that the benefits which do accrue to the developing countries will be very unevenly divided among them with the vast majority of developing countries gaining very little, if any, from the G.S.P.; and third, that the impact of preferential trade on donor-country production and employment is negligible even for a substantially expanded and liberalised G.S.P.

3

Developing Countries which Benefit from G.S.P.

A major prerequisite for putting the system of generalised preferences into operation is to determine which countries would be the recipients of the special tariff rates. Since the system is based on preferential treatment, at least two groups of countries must be identified – those whose exports would benefit and those whose exports would not.

The political process of dividing countries into such groups proved quite troublesome: multinational negotiations involving more than a hundred nations seldom reach clear-cut conclusions – especially when the negotiating forum is based on conflict rather than compromise.

Even the preference-giving countries could not agree among themselves on a common list of developing countries whose exports would qualify for G.S.P. tariff treatment. As might be expected, many of the donors had competing interests. For example, the United Kingdom wished the other donor countries to grant G.S.P. tariff treatment to all of the developing Commonwealth countries and territories including Hong Kong. But at the same time, if the United Kingdom granted G.S.P. tariff treatment to other developing countries, the value of Commonwealth preferences to the Commonwealth developing countries would be reduced as they would now have to compete in U.K. markets on the same basis as non-Commonwealth developing countries. Similar competing interests faced the E.E.C., which had special trading arrangements with a number of countries in Africa – the so-called Associated countries.*

THE PRINCIPLE OF SELF-ELECTION

The competing interests for some donor countries, coupled with the more liberal interests of others, finally led to an agreement that the G.S.P. should be a non-discriminatory system for all developing countries. But what is a developing country? How does a particular nation demonstrate that it should belong to the group of so-called 'beneficiaries'. To minimise the conflicts in negotiating a common list of beneficiaries, the donors initially agreed that countries would 'self-elect' themselves; thus any country could

---

* When the G.S.P. was first introduced by the E.E.C. in July 1971, the United Kingdom, Denmark and Ireland were not members of the E.E.C. Thus the Commonwealth developing countries and territories did not enjoy the special access to E.E.C. markets.

state that it was a developing country and thereby qualify itself as a beneficiary under the G.S.P. But this 'self-elect' concept soon led to difficulties as some of the more controversial countries claimed beneficiary status, for example Bulgaria, Cuba, Rumania, Taiwan and Yugoslavia (the United Kingdom also claimed such status for its territories, Hong Kong included). Because of these developments, and subsequent negotiation problems, it was further agreed that individual donor countries could decline to grant G.S.P. tariff status to any developing country on grounds 'which they hold compelling'.

Under this self-election concept, beneficiary status was claimed by the ninety-one countries then belonging to the Group of 77,* as well as Bulgaria, Cuba, Greece, Israel, Malta, Rumania, Spain, Taiwan and Turkey. Similar beneficiary status was claimed by Australia, the Netherlands, New Zealand and the United Kingdom for a number of their respective dependent territories.† But at the same time the beneficiary status of a number of countries was initially refused by the donor countries, each donor making its own decisions. Thus the beneficiary lists differ from donor to donor, with some developing countries receiving beneficiary status under some schemes and being denied such status under others. The general consensus was that all donors recognised, with only a few exceptions, the ninety-one countries then belonging to the Group of 77 as beneficiary developing countries. Most donor countries (except Finland and Japan) also initially granted beneficiary status to dependent territories. The problem countries were Communist countries (Bulgaria, Cuba and Rumania),‡ the relatively advanced developing countries of the Mediterranean basin (Greece, Israel, Malta, Spain and Turkey),§ Hong Kong, Israel and Taiwan.¶

Since the initial implementation of the G.S.P., the beneficiary lists have been gradually expanded and harmonised; but even today there exists a certain amount of discrimination among the developing countries based on economic as well as political factors. Hong Kong poses particular economic

---

* The ninety-one countries belonging to the Group of 77 included thirty-six in sub-Sahara Africa, sixteen in Asia and Oceania, two in Europe (Cyprus and Yugoslavia), twenty-three in Latin America and fourteen in the Middle East and Northern Africa. By 1974 five additional countries joined the Group, namely Bahrain, Bhutan, Cuba, Fiji and Qatar. Since then Bangladesh and a number of newly independent territories have joined, bringing the current membership to 114 developing countries.

† A number of dependent territories subsequently became independent nations; they now enjoy beneficiary status as countries rather than as territories.

‡ Yugoslavia, belonging to the Group of 77, was universally recognised as a beneficiary developing country from the start.

§ Portugal initially did not claim beneficiary status. Currently Portugal is a beneficiary of the scheme of Japan.

¶ Getting accurate information on the status of Taiwan is extremely difficult since its expulsion from the United Nations (more correctly, its seat has been transferred to the mainland government). Subsequent to this transfer, a political decision was made in the United Nations to eliminate any reference to Taiwan in all subsequent U.N. documents.

problems because of its competitiveness in world markets. When it is recognised as a beneficiary, special restrictions on G.S.P. trade are often imposed, as for example under the schemes of the E.E.C. and Japan. The Mediterranean countries are recognised by Japan (where transport costs provide a certain protective element for local industry) but not by the E.E.C. (due to a general Mediterranean policy based on bilateral trading agreements which is discussed later in this chapter). Taiwan poses a particularly sensitive political problem since the re-entry of mainland China into the arena of world politics. When the E.E.C. first introduced its scheme in July 1971, this problem was avoided, as the beneficiary list was limited to countries belonging to the Group of 77. Since Taiwan was not a member, the E.E.C. did not offend China by recognising Taiwan nor did they come under charges of discrimination by the Group of 77, which was a main negotiating force in UNCTAD.* Israel presented fewer problems at the time than exist today as the Arab countries flex their newly found muscle. Israel received beneficiary status from Austria, Japan, New Zealand, Sweden and Switzerland and was denied such status by the E.E.C. (primarily as a result of the Mediterranean policy), Finland and Norway. The final problem faced in drawing up the initial lists of beneficiary countries concerned the Communist countries of Eastern Europe, primarily Bulgaria and Rumania. Austria, Finland, Japan and New Zealand recognised both as beneficiaries; the E.E.C., Norway, Sweden and Switzerland recognised neither. Japan and Switzerland granted beneficiary status to Mongolia; and Finland and Sweden recognised both North Korea and North Vietnam as beneficiaries.

These special cases where particular developing countries are recognised as beneficiaries by some donors and not by others mean that the G.S.P. in total is definitely not the non-discriminatory system it was initially intended to be when the principle of self-election was adopted.† But the self-election concept had a second purpose, namely to guarantee that the selection of beneficiaries would not violate the principle of non-reciprocity. In the main the developing countries were granted G.S.P. status without reciprocity. The E.E.C. may have had some notions of using the G.S.P. to exert pressure on a number of Mediterranean countries but such a contention would be difficult

---

* The E.E.C.'s choice of using the Group of 77 as the initial beneficiary list was a neat way of avoiding other potential controversy as well. They did not offend the United States by recognising Cuba (though subsequently Cuba joined the Group of 77 and is now recognised as a beneficiary by most donor countries); they avoided the problems of East–West détente, as only Yugoslavia among the East European countries belonged to the Group of 77; and finally, the rab–Israeli controversey was avoided since Israel did not belong to the Group of 77.

† In the next chapter we will see that additional elements of discrimination have been built into several of the individual schemes. For example, the E.E.C. has a more limited list of beneficiary countries for textile products than for other items, and Japan has a special list of products for which Hong Kong exports do not qualify for G.S.P. tariff treatment.

to substantiate convincingly. During the recent past the E.E.C. has negotiated bilateral trade agreements with a number of Mediterranean countries
on a reciprocal basis. Under this policy, the E.E.C. seeks to establish economic co-operation involving trade, aid and technical assistance with all countries around the Mediterranean basin.

The agreements with Greece and Turkey aim ultimately at full membership in the E.E.C. customs union. Association agreements which stop short
of full membership have been negotiated with Morocco, Tunisia, Malta and
Cyprus;* and preferential trade agreements apply to Spain, Israel, Egypt and
Lebanon.† All of these agreements were negotiated on a reciprocal basis and
generally provide for preferential access to each other's markets. However,
they do not imply full reciprocity as the tariff concessions gained by the
E.E.C. are less favourable than those granted. The objective of the E.E.C. is
to increase the degree of economic interdependence among the nations of
this region. The E.E.C. may also have designs of eventual political influence.
Be that as it may, it is difficult to argue that G.S.P. beneficiary status, or lack
thereof, has been an important inducement for the Mediterranean countries
to enter into these agreements with the E.E.C.

RECIPROCITY UNDER THE U.S. G.S.P.

By far the strongest case of using the G.S.P. to elicit reciprocity from the
developing countries is found in the provisions of the U.S. scheme. The
authorising legislation does not identify the countries whose exports will
enjoy G.S.P. tariff treatment; instead it establishes a set of criteria to guide
the President in his deliberations for designating beneficiaries. The law also
treats the question of beneficiary designation over time, and may lead to
the suspension of such status for a particular country or a non-beneficiary
country subsequently receiving such status. Thus the behaviour of a developing country over time is taken into consideration by the United States in
deciding periodically whether a particular country should continue to enjoy
(or begin to enjoy) G.S.P. tariff treatment. Obviously the intent of such
conditions can only be to elicit economic or political behaviour on the part
of developing countries which is consistent with U.S. international economic
and political interests.

The criteria for beneficiary designation are, in general, negative, as they
specify conditions under which a particular developing country cannot be
designated a beneficiary.‡ Some of these conditions were brought up

* Of these countries only Malta does not enjoy G.S.P. beneficiary status under the E.E.C.
scheme.
† Egypt and Lebanon enjoy beneficiary status under the E.E.C.'s G.S.P.
‡ The law also contains a specified list of *developed* countries which cannot be designated,
namely Australia, Austria, Canada, Czechoslovakia, E.E.C. countries, Finland, East Germany,
Hungary, Iceland, Japan, Monaco, New Zealand, Norway, Poland, South Africa, Sweden,
Switzerland and the Soviet Union.

repeatedly by the United States in earlier negotiations on the G.S.P. and simply represent a consistent U.S. policy. But new conditions were added subsequent to the UNCTAD negotiations which are much more important, being sufficiently rigid that a number of developing countries which enjoy beneficiary status under other G.S.P. schemes will not do so under the U.S. scheme. The criteria apply to the following types of countries:

(1) communist countries;

(2) countries which participate in international commodity cartels such as OPEC;

(3) countries which grant 'reverse' preferences to the E.E.C., i.e. countries which admit imports from the E.E.C. under more favourable treatment than imports from the United States;

(4) countries which have nationalised or expropriated property owned by U.S. citizens or corporations without adequate compensation;

(5) countries which do not co-operate with the United States in combating illegal drug traffic; and

(6) countries which do not honour or enforce arbitration awards in favour of U.S. citizens or corporations which arise out of international investment disputes.

However, the law does permit the waiving of the latter three conditions if the President determines such action to be in the national economic interest. These conditions will be discussed in turn, treating first those criteria which are mandatory and cannot be waived, and second those which can be waived by the President in the national interest.

Criteria which cannot be waived

The first criteria refers to communist countries which are *a priori* excluded from enjoying preferences granted by the United States *unless:*

(1) the country's exports to the United States already enjoy M.F.N. treatment;

(2) such country is a contracting party to GATT and is a member of the I.M.F.; *and*

(3) such country is not dominated or controlled by international communism.

The wording of this provision is quite clear in that all three criteria must be met before the President can bestow beneficiary status on a communist country. Apart from the socialist countries of Eastern Europe included in the list of developed countries and thereby excluded as beneficiaries, the United States regards the following as communist countries: Albania, Bulgaria, the People's Republic of China, Cuba, the Democratic Republic of Vietnam, the Democratic People's Republic of Korea, Mongolia and Rumania. Of these countries only Rumania belongs to both GATT and the I.M.F.; Cuba belongs to GATT only; the remaining countries belong to neither of these international organisations.

U.S. trade policy regarding communist countries is heavily influenced by the current *détente* between the United States and the Soviet Union. Trade relations with the communist countries of Eastern Europe will not be fully normalised over-night. Instead there is a pseudo pecking-order by which trade will be liberalised gradually with communist countries one at a time. At present the United States considers a gradual normalisation of trade relations with Rumania as most consistent with the continuing *détente* with the Soviet Union. Pursuant to this policy an M.F.N. trade agreement has been negotiated with Rumania. After the U.S.–Rumania trade agreement was approved by Congress, Rumania was designated a beneficiary in the Executive Order implementing the U.S. G.S.P. which became effective on 1 January 1976.

No other communist country (for example Bulgaria or Cuba) is likely to gain beneficiary status soon, excepting of course Yugoslavia, which has already been so designated. Moreover, due to recent events in South-east Asia, South Vietnam and Cambodia were removed from the U.S. list of beneficiary developing countries prior to the formal implementation of the U.S. scheme.

The second criterion which prevents beneficiary designation concerns countries belonging to OPEC or participating in any other arrangement, 'the effect of which is to withhold supplies of vital commodity resources from international trade or to raise the price of such commodities to an unreasonable level', causing serious disruption of the world economy. The intent of this criterion is readily obvious. Further indications of the U.S. intent can be obtained from a 11 March 1975 statement by the U.S. delegation to the Organisation of American States:

> Apart from the apparent exclusion of OPEC members, we have perceived a widespread apprehension that the cartel provision of the Trade Act may be applied to Latin American countries which are members of or are contemplating membership in other producer organizations. The legislative history of the Trade Act makes it clear that this provision applies only to countries which participate in actions involving vital materials which cause serious disruption of the world economy. We do not consider this provision to be an impediment to legitimate economic action by raw material producing countries.
>
> I should caution delegates here, however, that a determination that an action by a producer association is not disruptive of the world economy and does not therefore require a with-drawal of GSP beneficiary status

should not be interpreted as a U.S. endorsement of such an action. We reserve the right to:
- press our legitimate concerns through normal diplomatic channels;
- defend ourselves against such egregious actions as politically motivated embargoes; and
- argue for and seek cooperative negotiated, bilateral or multilateral solutions to mutual problems, as opposed to unilateral measures.

However, there is one exception to this criterion in that the President may grant beneficiary status to a country falling under this provision if both the United States and the other country are party to a bilateral or multilateral trade agreement (which is not in violation) assuring the United States fair and equitable access at reasonable prices to supplies of articles of commerce important to the economic requirements of the United States and for which the latter does not have, or cannot easily develop, the necessary domestic productive capacity to supply its own requirements.

However, it is unlikely that any such agreements will be signed in the near future. Moreover, the U.S. Department of State is not taking any initiative in this direction because such agreements require guaranteed access to oil at *reasonable prices*. So long as the price of U.S. 'old oil' is controlled at a level below the world price, any trade agreement with a potential beneficiary developing country would have to incorporate a price noticeably below the OPEC price. Obviously, the OPEC countries would lose more from the reduced oil price than they would gain from U.S. tariff preferences, and therefore would be reluctant to enter into such an agreement. But if the United States decontrols the price of domestic oil, as President Ford has proposed, in the eyes of the State Department the United States would be 'legitimatizing' the OPEC price of oil. In this case the 'reasonable-price' clause would no longer pose a problem and the United States might take the initiative to negotiate trade agreements with a number of OPEC countries so they could benefit from U.S. tariff preferences. Since any such negotiations would be entered into only after considering the reaction of Congress, a number of OPEC countries would not be approached in this regard – primarily those OPEC countries which participated in the oil embargo, and any other OPEC country which would be denied U.S. G.S.P. treatment due to any other criteria such as the expropriation clause, which might affect Algeria, Libya and others, or the 'fishing-rights controversy' with Ecuador, caused by the seizure of a number of American fishing boats within Ecuador's self-proclaimed 200-mile territorial waters.

On the other hand, if a multilateral agreement is reached between oil consumer and producer nations, such an agreement could be used to justify granting G.S.P. treatment to all OPEC nations who meet the other criteria for beneficiary designation. Only in such an event should we expect any oil embargoing OPEC country to benefit from U.S. tariff preferences in the near future; and even in this case we should not expect all OPEC countries to immediately benefit from the U.S. G.S.P. as there are outstanding investment disputes with some of these countries.

This particular criterion is the single most important criterion, resulting initially in particular developing countries being refused participation in the U.S. G.S.P.; the OPEC provision alone affects Algeria, Ecuador, Gabon, Indonesia, Iran, Iraq, Kuwait, Libya, Nigeria, Qatar, Saudi Arabia, the United Arab Emirates and Venezuela. It has certainly generated the most intense reactions on the part of potential beneficiaries, as evidenced by recent pronouncements reported in the world press.

But it should be emphasised that these pronouncements are not falling on deaf ears. The U.S. administration is concerned with improving U.S.-developing-country relations, as can be seen from the following passage from President Ford's 11 April 1975 address to the U.S. Congress:

A vital element of our foreign policy is our relationship with the developing countries – in Africa, Asia and Latin America. These countries must know that America is a true and concerned friend, reliable both in word and deed.

As evidence of this friendship, I urge Congress to reconsider one provision of the 1974 Trade Act which has had an unfortunate and unintended impact on our relations with Latin America . . . . Under this legislation all members of OPEC were excluded from our generalized system of trade preferences. This unfortunately punished two South American friends – Ecuador and Venezuela – as well as other OPEC nations such as Nigeria and Indonesia, none of which participated in last year's oil embargo. . . .

I therefore endorse the amendments which have been introduced in the Congress to provide executive authority to waive all these restrictions in the trade act that are incompatible with our national interest.

As indicated in this speech Congress has before it a proposed revision of the 1974 Trade Act – the so-called Green Amendment – which would grant the President authority to waive this criterion if he determines that such action would be in the national economic interest of the United States *except* that he may not designate as a beneficiary developing country any nation which has participated, or is participating, in any action the effect of which is to withhold supplies of any vital commodity resource from international trade. The passage of this amendment would permit the President to waive the OPEC cartel criterion for those countries which did not participate in the oil embargo – Ecuador, Gabon, Indonesia, Iran, Nigeria and Venezuela.

President Ford and his administration were wholeheartedly in favour of the passage of this amendment. In its testimony before Congress favouring the Green amendment, the administration pointed out that:

the provision excluding OPEC members from GSP has come under sharp criticism from abroad as coercive, discriminatory and in violation of our international commitments. ... This provision also threatens to have serious adverse consequences on our relations with other countries, with which we are actively seeking to strengthen our relations. Other countries which did not participate in the oil embargo against us, have expressed to us their serious concern .... The adverse effect of automatic denial of GSP on our relations with the OPEC countries is in many cases wholly out of proportion to any advantage we might gain from excluding them. Tariff preferences are not appropriate policy instruments to influence the actions of petroleum exporters because of the negligible trade losses which result from the denial of preferences. On the other hand, denial of GSP can have an unfortunate effect of the atmosphere for constructive negotiations with these countries.

Many members of Congress concur with these sentiments. However, Congress as a body is still vitally concerned with the issues raised by the recent energy crises, including the oil embargo and the cartel price hike; and this issue is before them constantly as they deliberate on a new energy policy. Congress is so incensed that there is absolutely no possibility that the oil-embargoing countries will be granted beneficiary status in the near future – under any conditions. And their charity towards the other members of OPEC, who after all did participate in the oil price hike, causing extreme adjustment costs to several O.E.C.D. countries, is literally non-existent. Representative William Archer (Republican, Texas), a House Ways and Means Committee member, expressed a common sentiment by charging that Venezuela, Ecuador and others aided and abetted the embargo, and profited from it by asking $16 to $20 a barrel for their oil.[1] To make matters worse, Ecuador, a potential gainer under the Green amendment, has met with substantial public opposition in the United States due to its unilateral seizure of American fishing boats within its self-proclaimed 200-mile territorial waters.*

But OPEC is not the only problem under this criterion – it also refers to any cartel arrangement the effect of which is to withhold supplies of commodity resources vital to the world economy or to raise prices of such commodities to an unreasonable level. Whereas at present no developing country is denied beneficiary status due to a non-OPEC cartel arrangement, a few other cartels (bauxite, copper and iron ore) are under scrutiny by the U.S. administration. Bauxite came to be an issue due to the recent increase in export taxes levied by Jamaica, but there is no formal cartel arrangement. On the other hand, the copper cartel has taken a formal decision to cut

---

* All OPEC countries were excluded from the beneficiary list contained in the Executive Order implementing the U.S. G.S.P. which became effective on 1 January 1976.

exports by 10 per cent over a six-month period. However, in light of the current world-wide recession copper prices have fallen so no world price or supplies impact has yet been felt.

There can be little doubt, however, that the U.S. Congress is vitally concerned and would use its G.S.P. to coerce 'responsible economic behaviour' on the part of the developing countries. The administration, however, can be expected to moderate this coercive action by facilitating the widest possible latitude for beneficiary-country behaviour while appeasing congressional concern – certainly this is not an enviable position.

The third criterion concerns the long-standing issue of 'reverse' preferences. The law precludes the President from designating as a beneficiary any developing country which

accords preferential treatment to the products of a developed country, other than the U.S., which has, or is likely to have, a significant adverse effect on U.S. commerce, unless the President has received assurances satisfactory to him that such preferential treatment will be eliminated before 1 January 1976, or that action will be taken before 1 January 1976, to assure that there will be no such significant adverse effect.

The United States has consistently opposed 'reverse' preferences throughout the negotiations on the G.S.P. and has consistently stated that developing countries *either receiving or granting* 'reverse' preferences would be excluded from enjoying U.S. tariff preferences from the outset. Gradually the U.S. position became more flexible. Under an earlier version of the 1974 Trade Act (the Trade Reform Act of 1973) a developing country was permitted to enjoy special preferences but could not grant 'reverse' preferences unless it provided assurances that such 'reverse' preferences would be eliminated by 1 January 1976.

The final wording of the 1974 Trade Act carries this liberalisation two steps forward. First, the full elimination of 'reverse' preferences by 1 January 1976 is no longer necessary for a developing country to enjoy G.S.P. tariff treatment provided assurances are given that action will be taken such that 'reverse' preferences will not have a significant adverse effect on U.S. commerce.

This last point involves the second major liberalisation. 'Reverse' preferences are now an issue only when they have, or are likely to have, a *significant adverse effect* on U.S. commerce. The determination of a 'significant adverse effect' is based on: (1) an examination of products under a 'reverse' preference agreement in which the United States is competitive in world markets; (2) the volume of 'reverse' preference trade; and (3) the margin of tariff preference against U.S. exports. Since most developing countries involved in the 'reverse' preference issue are by and large not major markets for U.S. products, this rewording of the 'reverse' preference criterion is likely to reduce significantly the number of developing countries to be barred from U.S. preferential tariff treatment due to this criterion.

When the issue of 'reverse' preferences first arose, it was mainly of concern to those developing countries in Africa which were associated with the E.E.C. via the Yaoundé and Arusha Conventions and the Algeria, Tunisia and Morocco trade agreements. Morocco, however, has extended its 'preferred' tariff treatment to all nations and is therefore not discriminating; Morocco has already been designated a beneficiary. The E.E.C. association agreement has recently been renegotiated to accommodate the newly associating Commonwealth countries of Africa, the Caribbean and Indian and Pacific Oceans as required by U.K. entry into the E.E.C. Under the new association agreement – the Lomé Convention – the forty-six developing countries of Africa, the Caribbean and Indian and Pacific Oceans (including those countries which were already associated) are no longer required to grant 'reverse' preferences to the E.E.C. Operating under the assumption that these countries will not be granting 'reverse' preferences after 1 January 1976, the President has designated them as beneficiaries under the U.S. G.S.P. But if these countries choose to grant the E.E.C. 'reverse' preferences, the administration will be required by the 1974 Trade Act to re-examine their beneficiary status. Presumably, the overwhelming majority would still gain beneficiary status on the ground that their 'reverse' preferences have no significant adverse effect on U.S. commerce. Tunisia has also been designated a beneficiary by the President on the *assumption* that its 'reverse' preferences would be eliminated before 1 January 1976. If this assumption proves to be incorrect, the President will be required to re-examine the case; the finding of any significant adverse effect on U.S. commerce would require the President to remove Tunisia from the list of beneficiary countries. Of the traditional 'reverse' preference countries only Algeria has been denied beneficiary status – but on the grounds of its membership in OPEC rather than 'reverse' preferences.

In addition to the associated countries, the E.E.C. has negotiated 'reverse' preference trade agreements with a number of other countries under its so-called Mediterranean policy – Cyprus, Egypt, Greece, Israel, Lebanon, Malta, Portugal, Spain and Turkey. The administration is currently in the process of determining the effect on U.S. commerce of these agreements. To date, determinations of no adverse effect have been reached for Egypt, Lebanon and Malta; consequently, these countries have been designated as beneficiary developing countries. However, their status is under continual monitoring especially in regard to their trade in agricultural products. A finding of significant adverse effect has been reached regarding Israel; Israel has been notified of this finding and of its consequences. Thus, unless Israel provides formal assurances that action will be taken by 1 January 1976 to eliminate 'reverse' preferences or to assure that the significant adverse effects on U.S. commerce is alleviated, Israel will not be designated a beneficiary developing country. However, Israel has strong congressional support for designation as a beneficiary and is likely to gain beneficiary status somehow.

No formal finding has yet been reached with respect to the 'reverse' preferences of Cyprus, Greece, Portugal, Spain and Turkey. In all likelihood some significant adverse effects will be identified for each of these five Mediterranean countries.

Thus the 'reverse' preference provision will continue to play a substantial role in the U.S. G.S.P. First, it will continually hang over the heads of Egypt, Lebanon, Malta and Tunisia; hence they must guard against such preferences causing significant adverse effects on U.S. commerce. Second, it will prohibit Israel – and in all likelihood Cyprus, Greece, Portugal, Spain and Turkey as well – from enjoying U.S. tariff preferences *unless* they take action to protect the trading interests of the United States.* In this regard the Congress emphasised that

> One of the purposes of generalized tariff preferences is to provide an alternative to the proliferation of special preferential trading arrangements between the European Community and the developing countries in Africa, the Caribbean and around the Mediterranean, which often involve 'reverse' preferences which discriminate against exports of the U.S. This requirement is intended to provide increased pressure on developed and developing countries to remove 'reverse' preferences within a reasonable period of time or at least to modify them in such a way that U.S. trade is not adversely affected.[2]

Again the intent of the inclusion of this criterion as a prerequisite for beneficiary status is clear. As emphasised in the above statement reflecting congressional attitudes, U.S. preferences are intended to elicit from developing countries particular economic or political behaviour favourable to U.S. interests. The U.S. system of tariff preferences is therefore coupled with implicit requests for reciprocity on the part of those developing countries to be designated as beneficiaries.

Criteria that are subject to waiver

In the previous section, three negative criteria were discussed which prevent the President from bestowing beneficiary status on particular countries. Procedurally, the President must *determine* that each country he wishes to designate as a beneficiary developing country does not violate any of these criteria. Upon such determination, the President notifies Congress of his intent to so designate the particular country and communicates his *considerations* for designation. If the President determines that a country meets the

---

* Cyprus, Israel and Turkey were designated as beneficiaries in the Executive Order implementing the U.S. G.S.P. which became effective on 1 January 1976.

criteria, he simply informs Congress of the particular paragraphs of the 1974 Trade Act which relate to the particular country – but he need not communicate the specific facts used in reaching his determination.

The three criteria to be discussed below – relating to (1) expropriation, (2) illegal drug traffic, and (3) arbitral awards – are subject to waiver by the President if he determines that such designation would be in the national economic interest of the United States. If the President chooses to exercise this waiver, he must report such determination to Congress *together with his reasons* for such determination. Thus Congress wants to know exactly what facts were used by the President in determining that a national economic-interest waiver is justified; note also that the waiver is on the grounds of 'national *economic* interest' rather than the more general 'national interest'. Presumably, political or foreign-policy interests are insufficient to justify a waiver.

This procedural distinction between (1) determining that a country meets the criteria so that the President simply reports to Congress the final determination with his considerations (rather than facts), and (2) exercising the waiver requiring the President to report to Congress the factual reasons used in reaching his determination, has already proved an important issue in the President's efforts to designate the initial list of beneficiary developing countries. On 13 January 1975 President Ford notified Congress of his intention to designate beneficiaries under the U.S. G.S.P. That list contained four developing countries – Gabon, the People's Republic of Yemen, Somalia and Uganda – which were in possible violation of one or more of the criteria for beneficiary designation. The President attempted to exercise the national economic-interest waiver 'for all countries to which it applies' on the procedural ground that it would facilitate International Trade Commission efforts to investigate the list of eligible products for the likely impact of tariff preferences on the U.S. economy (see Chapter 4 below). In this waiver the President did not identify the countries to which it applied nor did he give the factual reasons relating each country's inclusion in the beneficiary list to the national economic interest. Congress objected; the President withdrew his notification; and on 24 March 1975 he again wrote to Congress stating his intention to designate a number of countries as beneficiary developing countries; this newer list did not contain Gabon, the People's Republic of Yemen, Somalia and Uganda. The national economic-interest waiver was not exercised with respect to any country. It is fair to say that any President will be reluctant to exercise this waiver unless he can establish a defensible causal tie between the particular country to be designated and the national *economic* interest in the United States.

In this light the following three criteria should be considered as mandatory criteria. The normal latitude which the President takes in administering the law will most likely be taken in his determination that a particular country meets the criteria. Thus he can report to Congress this determination together with his considerations – he need not report the facts used in reaching his determination.

As mentioned above there are three criteria which are subject to waiver relating to (1) expropriation, (2) illegal drug traffic, and (3) arbitral awards. The last two have not prevented any developing country from being designated a beneficiary; and due to the latitude given the President in administering the first, it prevented beneficiary designation in only two of the twenty-one cases to which it applied. It must be recognised that the administration, which has the responsibility for foreign policy, is sincerely interested in maximising the list of beneficiary countries; but in so doing the administration cannot afford to alienate Congress. It is to appease Congress that the expropriation criterion was inserted in the Trade Reform Bill of 1973 (the earlier version of the 1974 Trade Act); Congress itself took the initiative to amend the Trade Reform Bill to include the 'illegal drug traffic' and 'arbitral awards' criteria. These three criteria will be discussed in turn.

The first criterion subject to waiver involves those developing countries which:

(1) have nationalised, expropriated or otherwise seized ownership or control of property owned by a U.S. citizen, corporation, partnership or association which is 50 per cent or more beneficially owned by U.S. citizens;

(2) have taken steps to repudiate or nullify an existing contract or agreement . . . the effect of which is to nationalise, expropriate or otherwise seize ownership or control; or

(3) have imposed or enforced taxes or other extractions, restrictive maintenance or operational conditions, or other measures the effect of which is to nationalise, expropriate or otherwise seize ownership or control.

No such country shall benefit from U.S. tariff preferences *unless* the President determines, and promptly communicates such determination to Congress, that:

(1) prompt, adequate and effective compensation has or is being made;

(2) good faith negotiations to provide such compensation are in progress or other steps to discharge such an obligation are being taken; or

(3) the investment dispute has been submitted to arbitration under the provisions of the Convention for the Settlement of Investment Disputes, or in another mutually agreed upon forum.

To date the United States has investigated twenty-one different outstanding investment disputes concerning potential beneficiary developing countries; eighteen of the countries involved have been designated by the

President as beneficiary developing countries pursuant to his notification to Congress on 24 March 1975. This notification states in part:

I hereby determine on the basis of a review conducted by interested agencies of the Executive Branch of each of the relevant investment disputes that, in the case of each country listed below, *good faith negotiations* to provide prompt, adequate, and effective compensation under the applicable provisions of international law are in progress, or such country is otherwise *taking steps to discharge its obligations* under international law (emphasis added).

Afghanistan	Ethiopia
Argentina	India
Bangladesh	Morocco
Bolivia	Pakistan
Central African Republic	Sri Lanka
Congo (Brazzaville)	Sudan
Dahomey	Syria
Egypt	Tanzania
El Salvador	Zaire

There were, however, three other cases for which no such determination was made; of the three countries involved, the People's Republic of Yemen and Uganda have not been designated as beneficiary developing countries although they are still under consideration. Some recent steps are being taken toward settlement of the investment disputes regarding Uganda, so it is quite possible that this country will soon be designated as a beneficiary developing country. The third case is more problematic since the United States does not have diplomatic relations with the People's Republic of Yemen. Somalia was designated a beneficiary in the Executive Order implementing the U.S. G.S.P. which became effective on 1 January 1976.

One final comment: the administration is likely to continue to interpret this criterion as liberally as possible by designating as a beneficiary any country which it can assure Congress is making any reasonable attempts to enter into good-faith negotiations. The United States recognises the rights of sovereign nations to guide and control their domestic economies; but it is the policy of the United States that if expropriation of a foreign-owned company is deemed important by a developing country, some form of compensation is in order. However, it is unfortunate that the G.S.P. is being used as a policy instrument by the United States in its attempt to conduct such policy. This is like eating peas with a knife; while it may be somewhat useful, an alternative instrument would in all likelihood be much more effective.

The second criterion subject to waiver is aimed at eliciting developing-country co-operation in the fight to prevent narcotic and other illegal drugs from entering the United States unlawfully. This clause was not included in the earlier version of the law but was added by amendment in the Senate version. It was probably the result of one or more Senators being concerned about illegal drug traffic and noting that the problem-exporting countries – primarily Turkey and certain Latin American nations – were potential beneficiaries of the U.S. G.S.P. Its inclusion in the 1974 Trade Act was not sought by the U.S. Executive and it is unlikely that this clause will prevent many developing countries from enjoying U.S. tariff preferences. The drafting of the law leaves the President substantial leeway since the potential beneficiary developing country is only required to 'take adequate steps to cooperate with the U.S. to prevent . . .'. To date no developing country has been denied beneficiary status due to this criterion.

The third and final criterion subject to waiver concerns arbitral awards arising out of investment disputes. The 1974 Trade Act states:

> the President shall not designate any country a beneficiary developing country . . . if such country fails to act in good faith in recognizing as binding or in enforcing arbitral awards in favor of [a U.S. party] which has been made [through an arbitration] to which the parties involved have submitted their dispute.

This criterion is obviously related to the earlier criterion concerning the nationalisation or expropriation of property owned by U.S. citizens. But this criterion was first introduced in the Senate version of the 1974 Trade Act whereas the nationalisation criterion appeared in the Trade Reform Bill as originally submitted to Congress by the President. In talking to various government officials, I learned that this criterion was introduced as a result of an existing investment dispute between a U.S. corporation and the Government of India. This investment dispute, under mutual consent, was submitted to arbitration on the understanding that the outcome could be appealed in Indian courts. The arbitration procedure resulted in an award to the corporation; but the case was appealed by the government of India in Indian courts, a notoriously time-consuming process. It was reported to me that the U.S. corporation is being represented by a U.S. law firm, and that one of the firm's partners is the U.S. Senator who is responsible for introducing the arbitral awards amendment to the Trade Act of 1974.

To date no developing country, including India, has been denied beneficiary status as a result of this criterion. It is hoped that this experience will continue in the future, making this clause, in effect, a dead-letter criterion.

The special case of Hong Kong

As with most preference-giving countries, the United States fears that preferential tariff treatment for Hong Kong may result in undue import displacement. Such a fear is sufficiently widespread both in and out of government that Hong Kong was not initially designated a beneficiary. Based on the criteria for beneficiary designation – as contained in the 1974 Trade Act, explicitly or implicitly including the 'sense of Congress' – Hong Kong meets all of the criteria for designation as a beneficiary developing country. However, Hong Kong designation was challenged on the rationale that Hong Kong is not a developing country from the international trade point of view – Hong Kong is already competitive in world markets and therefore does not need tariff preferences. Moreover, in extending preferences the President is required to have due regard for 'the extent to which other major developed countries are undertaking a *comparable* effort to assist developing countries'. Hong Kong has certainly received 'special' G.S.P. treatment by the E.E.C. and Japan through the imposition of special ceilings on preferential imports or through a substantially reduced G.S.P. product list. The U.S. scheme does not provide much scope for the 'special' treatment of any beneficiary; only when a particular beneficiary is affected by the 'competitive-need' formula will its eligible products list differ from that of other beneficiaries.

In light of the domestic opposition to Hong Kong's designation as a beneficiary, the U.S. administration must treat this case with great concern. The administration does argue that the G.S.P. scheme does contain sufficient measures to protect domestic interests and thus is in favour of designating Hong Kong as a beneficiary developing country *at the appropriate time.**

Based on the above criteria the President has designated a number of countries as beneficiary developing countries. Due to the legislative efforts to revise the criteria for beneficiary designation and to other factors entering into presidential determination, a number of countries have been identified which have not yet been designated as beneficiaries but are still under consideration for such designation.

Those developing countries recognised as beneficiaries by one or more preference-giving countries but not so designated under the U.S. G.S.P. are listed below according to the primary criteria by which they are currently denied beneficiary status.

(1) Communist countries – Bulgaria, Cambodia, Cuba, the Democratic People's Republic of Korea, Democratic Republic of Vietnam (including South Vietnam) and Mongolia;

(2) Countries belonging to OPEC: (i) these which participated in the oil embargo – Algeria, Iraq, Kuwait, Libya, Qatar, Saudi Arabia, and the

* Given the congressional favouritism for designating Israel (with an annual *per capita* income of some $2400), the U.S. administration is likely to include Hong Kong on the same list of countries to be designated as Israel. The intent is to minimise the public reaction at designating Hong Kong. (Note: Both Hong Kong and Israel were included in the Executive Order implementing the U.S. G.S.P. which became effective on 1 January 1976.)

United Arab Emirates; (ii) those which did not participate in the oil embargo, and, therefore, come under the Green Amendment – Ecuador, Gabon, Indonesia, Iran, Nigeria and Venezuela;

(3) Countries granting 'reverse' preferences – Greece, Portugal and Spain;

(4) Countries which nationalised or expropriated property owned by a U.S. citizen or corporation without compensation – the People's Democratic Republic of Yemen and Uganda;

(5) No country was denied beneficiary designation due to the 'illegal drug traffic' criterion; and

(6) No country was denied beneficiary designation due to the 'arbitral awards' criterion.

Two points should be noted, however. First, the status of a number of these non-beneficiary countries is subject to change after the initial implementation of the U.S. G.S.P. without the need for any congressional action; Greece, Portugal, Spain, the People's Democratic Republic of Yemen and Uganda are all likely candidates for beneficiary designation; and second, even if the OPEC-cartel criterion were to be modified by congressional action, a number of the countries so affected would still face problems regarding beneficiary designation due to unresolved investment disputes.

E.E.C. ASSOCIATES AND THE G.S.P.

Up to this point the discussion has concentrated on those developing countries which have been discriminated against or who are expected to grant some form of reciprocity in return for G.S.P. favours. There are, however, a number of beneficiaries who receive access to E.E.C. markets, which is more favourable than that accorded under the G.S.P. Such treatment is a carry-over from earlier E.E.C. agreements with a number of countries in Africa, i.e. the newly independent French territories which participated in the Yaoundé and Arusha agreements. After the United Kingdom joined the E.E.C., U.K. Commonwealth preferences were phased out. But at the same time the trade interests of the Commonwealth developing countries were taken into consideration by the E.E.C. in formulating the enlarged E.E.C.'s international economic policy regarding the developing countries. Under this new policy, many Commonwealth developing countries were invited to associate with the E.E.C.* As a result the association agreement was renegotiated to include a total of forty-six developing countries in Africa, the Caribbean, and the Indian and Pacific Oceans (including the old E.E.C. Associates under the Yaoundé and Arusha agreements as well as the newly associating Common-

---

* A few of the Commonwealth developing countries were not offered association status; these so-called 'outer seven' are Bangladesh, Hong Kong, India, Malaysia, Pakistan, Singapore and Sri Lanka.

wealth developing countries). This new Lomé Convention provides these countries with duty-free access to E.E.C. markets covering a wide range of industrial and agricultural products as well as financial and technical assistance.

The existence of these special arrangements have significant implications for the G.S.P. In the first place, even though these countries have G.S.P. beneficiary status, they do not really benefit since their access to E.E.C. markets is more favourable under the association agreement. Thus for all practical purposes these countries are not beneficiaries under the E.E.C. G.S.P. scheme.

Second, as a result of the G.S.P., the associated countries must now share their preferential tariff access to E.E.C. markets with other developing countries. Consequently, the value of their association status is being eroded by the G.S.P.; but this erosion is limited. The E.E.C. took this relationship into account in designing its G.S.P. scheme and excluded or severely restricted G.S.P. trade in products of export interest to the associated countries. For example, G.S.P. tariff treatment does not apply to any industrial raw material, many of which are exported by the African Associates. In fact, less than 10 per cent of these Associates' exports to the E.E.C. of products covered by the association agreement are also covered by the G.S.P. scheme.[3] In addition, those few agricultural items included in the E.E.C. scheme receive only minor tariff cuts under the G.S.P. In contrast, under the association agreement the agricultural items covered qualify for more substantial tariff cuts. Thus, even when G.S.P. tariff treatment applies to an agricultural item of export interest to an associated country, there remains a substantial preferential tariff margin in favour of the Associate. And finally, the E.E.C. scheme places ceiling limits on E.E.C. imports which receive G.S.P. tariff treatment; no such ceilings exist under the association agreement.

THE LEAST DEVELOPED AND THE G.S.P.

The last issue concerning particular developing countries under the G.S.P. relates to the so-called 'Least Developed Among the Developing Countries'.[4] Interest in these countries arose after recognition of the wide disparity in the levels of economic development among the developing countries. The desire is to devise and implement special measures in favour of these countries to enhance the opportunities for economic development.

Early during the negotiations for the G.S.P. it was recognised that the least developed were unlikely to benefit much from a pure preferential tariff programme which was limited to manufactured products. Consequently, it was agreed that the donor countries should introduce, within the context of the G.S.P., special measures in favour of these countries. But in so agreeing, the delegates stipulated further that:

(1) such special measures would be supplementary and should not prevent the least developed from benefiting from the normal G.S.P. as well; and

(2) such special measures would not interfere with the ability of other developing countries to benefit from the G.S.P.

When the G.S.P. was first introduced in late 1971 and early 1972, the schemes contained no supplementary special measures for the least developed. In fact, very little opportunity existed to help them via a policy dealing solely with trade. In the first place, over three-quarters of the least developed country export earnings are derived from products which enter the donor countries free of duty under M.F.N. conditions. The remaining trade involves agricultural commodities and certain industrial raw materials – the major suppliers of which are other developing countries – that are considered import-sensitive by the donor countries. Thus the donors argue that the inclusion in the G.S.P. of most of these products would result in imports (from non-least developed beneficiaries) sufficient to disrupt domestic markets. The donors would be willing to grant G.S.P. tariff treatment on such products only if the least developed were the only beneficiaries, i.e. only if the donors could discriminate among the developing countries. But such discriminatory treatment violates one of the main corner-stones of the G.S.P., the principle of non-discrimination; and this non-discrimination principle is also included in the UNCTAD resolutions calling for special measures in favour of the least developed. But just how can 'special measures in favour of' the least developed be at the same 'non-discriminatory'? There seems to be an inherent conflict which is in all likelihood responsible for the fact that little has been done for the least developed within the context of the G.S.P. What is needed by the least developed is newly created export capacity, meaning financial and technical assistance – and this is obviously not a 'trade policy' within the context of the G.S.P.

4

Product Coverage

The primary objective of the G.S.P. is to expand exports and export earnings of developing countries by stimulating donor-country imports of manufactured products from them, the incentive being provided by preferential tariff rates. Before judging its effectiveness, however, this programme must be placed in its proper perspective. First and foremost it is a tariff policy, and therefore can contribute to increased exports of only those products subject to duty. There is no scope within the context of the G.S.P. for assisting the export prospects of products which currently enter donor countries free of duty on an M.F.N. basis.

The second major element is that the G.S.P. was envisaged to offer an alternative source of export earnings to the developing countries. Hitherto the developing countries have depended heavily on exports of primary agricultural commodities and industrial raw materials. This excessive dependence has posed a twofold problem: cyclical market conditions normally resulted in rather large swings in commodity prices and consequently export earnings; and structural conditions have resulted in relatively slow-growing markets for commodities due to low income elasticities for agricultural commodities and the development of synthetic substitutes for industrial raw materials. In contrast, international markets for manufactured products have been growing rapidly and steadily – except possibly for the recent period of world-wide recession; but even in this latter case, the downturn in markets for industrial raw materials is much more extreme than for finished manufactures.

Thus a major objective of the G.S.P. was to provide a stimulus for a shift of productive effort in developing countries away from primary commodities and toward manufacturing. (This is not to suggest that primary production should be completely phased-out but rather that it would rationally be based on national factor endowments and international comparative advantage.) This dichotomy between industrial and commodity products was built into the G.S.P. by agreements that the preferential tariffs would apply to manufactured products only. In implementing this agreement the donors interpreted manufactured products as including only industrial manufactures and semi-manufactures; processed and semi-processed agricultural and fishery items were considered to fall outside the scope of the G.S.P. This treatment of agricultural and fishery items was also heavily influenced by the existence of domestic agricultural support programmes in the developed countries, for example the U.S. price-support system coupled with import quotas, or the E.E.C. system of variable levies on imports to guarantee high domestic farm prices.

At the same time it was recognised that many developing countries would be unable to benefit from a G.S.P. limited entirely to non-agricultural products. To appease these countries a token list of agricultural and fishery items were initially included. A factor that tends to limit the value of G.S.P. tariff treatment for these products is that the preferential tariff margins are sometimes quite minor. When the E.E.C. first introduced its G.S.P. scheme, such items qualified for an average 4 percentage points of duty reduction, i.e. the average duty was reduced from 16 to 12 per cent.

DEVELOPING-COUNTRY EXPORTS AND THE G.S.P.

Once it is recognised that the G.S.P. cannot apply to duty-free exports and will not apply to the bulk of agricultural and fishery exports, we find the scope of this programme to be somewhat limited. The significance of these exceptions is easily highlighted by examining the correspondence between developing-country exports and the products which come under the G.S.P. provisions. Based on 1970 trade flows, over half (58 per cent) of the developing-country exports to the eighteen donor countries of the West entered free of duty. This is due to the fact that developing countries have traditionally exported a significant volume of industrial raw materials, most of which are not subject to duty. The dutiable agricultural- and fishery-product exclusion accounts for an additional 14 per cent of developing-country exports. These two product classes combined account for just under three-quarters of developing-country exports. Thus beneficiary exports of manufactured goods *potentially eligible* for G.S.P. tariff treatment account for roughly one-quarter of their trade with the donor countries. And this is not the end of the story – instead it is only the beginning.

When the G.S.P. was being negotiated, prior to its introduction in 1971, it was agreed that the donors would take whatever safeguard measures they deemed necessary to protect their domestic markets from undue disruption that might be caused by G.S.P. imports. In so doing, the donors introduced a number of limitations into their individual G.S.P. schemes. Each decided to protect domestic producers of 'import-sensitive' products (mainly textiles, leather and petroleum-based products). Most donors simply excluded such products from G.S.P. treatment.

The E.E.C. excluded dutiable industrial raw materials primarily to accommodate the export interests of the African nations associated with the E.E.C. They protected E.E.C. textile producers by establishing three distinct product classes; the list of developing countries whose exports received G.S.P. tariff treatment varied by product class. The product classes and corresponding beneficiary developing countries are as follows:

(1) Cotton textiles subject to GATT-negotiated 'Long Term Arrangement Regarding Trade in Cotton Textiles' (L.T.A.) and substitute products: beneficiaries are those developing countries belonging to the Group of 77 *and* signatories to the L.T.A. or those which bilaterally agreed with the E.E.C. to behave as though they were signatories* – in 1971 this group consisted of Colombia, Egypt, India, Jamaica, South Korea, Mexico and Pakistan. In 1974 the expired L.T.A. was superseded by the 'Arrangement Regarding International Trade in Textiles', which covers man-made fibers as well. Additional developing countries observe the new arrangement; thus the E.E.C. beneficiary list for these textiles now includes Afghanistan, Argentina, Bangladesh, Colombia, Egypt, El Salvador, India, Indonesia, Jamaica, South Korea, Malaysia, Mexico, Pakistan, the Philippines and Thailand;

(2) Other textiles and footwear: beneficiaries include only countries belonging to the Group of 77, which is a means of excluding dependent territories – primarily Hong Kong; and

(3) All other G.S.P. products, including manufactures, semi-manufactures and agricultural and fishery items: beneficiaries are countries belonging to the Group of 77 and dependent territories, i.e. the full list of E.E.C. beneficiaries as described in the previous chapter.

The industrial products thereby excluded by the E.E.C. account for roughly one-third of E.E.C. imports of dutiable industrial products from the beneficiary developing countries.

Japan did not introduce such an elaborate technique for excluding import-sensitive products†. But exclusions were made none the less, covering textiles, leather and petroleum products, and a few additional items such as plywood, raw silk, woven silk fabric, and gelatine and glues derived from bones. These exclusions account for *three-quarters* of Japan's imports of dutiable industrial products from the beneficiaries – the bulk of such trade involves petroleum.

The remaining major donor, the United States, has the widest range of pure exclusions. The authorising legislation prohibits the granting of G.S.P. tariff treatment on the following items:

(1) textiles and apparel articles which are subject to textile agreements under the new L.T.A.;

(2) footwear;

(3) any article subject to national security action – petroleum and petroleum products;

---

* The significance of limiting G.S.P. tariff treatment to those beneficiaries which abide by the L.T.A. is that under the L.T.A. these countries have agreed to 'voluntarily' limit their exports. Thus G.S.P. tariff incentives cannot have a stimulating effect on beneficiary exports.

† The E.E.C., in the UNCTAD forum, maintains that its G.S.P. scheme covers all manufactured and semi-manufactured industrial products *without* exception. The E.E.C. further maintains that it does not discriminatorily exclude certain developing countries with respect to textiles; these countries exclude themselves by not abiding by the new L.T.A. arrangement.

(4) watches;

(5) import-sensitive electronic articles;

(6) import-sensitive steel articles;

(7) import-sensitive glass products;

(8) any article subject to an escape clause under the Trade Expansion Act of 1962, or import-relief action under the Trade Act of 1974;* and

(9) any other article which the President determines to be import-sensitive in the context of the G.S.P.

It is interesting, however, that many of these excluded articles were not defined in the Trade Act of 1974, for example import-sensitive electronic, steel and glass products. These products had to be subsequently defined through the following political processes:

(1) investigations by the International Trade Commission to determine the likely effect of G.S.P. tariff treatment on U.S. production, employment and consumption of like or competitive articles;

(2) public hearings where interested producer, worker and consumer groups could express their views concerning the U.S. G.S.P.; and

(3) advice supplied by the executive branches of government – the Departments of Agriculture, Commerce, Labor, State, Treasury, the Special Representative for Trade Negotiations, and so on.

Eventually a list of product exclusions was decided upon by the U.S. government; it is not surprising that a number of major products of export interest for the developing countries were excluded from the U.S. scheme – such exclusion accounts for just under three-quarters of U.S. imports of dutiable industrial products from the developing countries. On paper the U.S. coverage in the agricultural and fishery sectors is by far the most impressive of the major donors; just over one-half of U.S. imports of dutiable agricultural and fishery products from beneficiaries fall under the U.S. scheme. However, as will be shown in the next chapter, much of this trade will not receive G.S.P. tariff treatment due to the U.S. 'competitive need' criteria.

To emphasise the correspondence between products which qualify for G.S.P. tariff treatment and products exported by the developing countries, Table 4.1 presents major donor-country imports from the beneficiary developing countries, sub-divided by product group and tariff treatment. In total only 13 per cent of developing-country exports to the donor countries

---

* Articles currently subject to escape-clause action are of minor export interest to the developing countries. Since no new escape-clause action will be taken (the escape clause has been superseded by the import-relief measures specified under the Trade Act of 1974), this clause is a dead letter as far as the U.S. G.S.P. is concerned. However, import-relief action under the new Act can be very significant (see Chapter 5 below).

TABLE 4.1

Donor-country imports from beneficiaries
(1970 in billions of U.S. dollars)

Donor importer	Total imports	Dutiable imports	Covered by G.S.P.
E.E.C.	18·2	5·5	1·4
United States	7·8	4·5	1·7
Japan	6·9	3·9	0·8
Other donors	2·9	1·1	0·5
Total	35·8	15·0	4·4

SOURCE: UNCTAD Secretariat calculations, reported in documents *TD/B/C.5/22* and *TD/B/C.5/38*.

consist of products which qualify for G.S.P. tariff treatment. But to be fair to the donors, duty-free items obviously fall outside the scope of the G.S.P.; however, taking this into account still results in G.S.P. schemes that cover only 30 per cent of the donors' dutiable imports from the beneficiaries. The reasons for this poor correspondence between actual trade flows and the G.S.P. schemes' product coverage is that the bulk of dutiable agricultural and fishery items are excluded from the G.S.P. as are many industrial products of proven export interest to developing countries, such as textiles and leather products. These exclusions are highlighted in the summary of donor-country trade with the benefeficiaries (see Table 4.2). In conclusion, the G.S.P. schemes do not include a number of products which, at least today, are important sources of export earnings for the beneficiary developing countries. And thus the importance of the G.S.P. as a commercial policy for developing countries depends upon the strength of the incentives for reallocating productive effort.

TABLE 4.2

Trade-flow summary	Value ($ billion)	Share (per cent)
All products	35·8	100
Products admitted duty-free under M.F.N. tariffs	20·7	58
Dutiable agricultural and fishery products not covered by G.S.P.	5·1	14
Dutiable industrial products excluded by G.S.P. to protect domestic producers	5·5	15
Products covered by G.S.P.	4·5	13

G.S.P. TARIFF INCENTIVES

These data, although somewhat discouraging, are not sufficient to conclude that the G.S.P. offers no potential. A multitude of factors, including the structure of tariff rates in the industrial nations, have created the incentives that produced the current pattern of trade. The G.S.P. changes the structure of tariff rates and, consequently, the incentives. It is not unreasonable to anticipate that this change in incentives will bring about at least some reallocation of industrial production favouring the developing countries. Since the industrial markets for manufactured goods have been growing rapidly, it was agreed that by emphasising precisely these goods, the historical dependence on exports of primary products could be reduced, thereby improving the prospects of earning badly needed foreign exchange. Even for the resource-rich developing countries, industrial diversification is an important prerequisite for economic development. The preferential reduction of tariff rates should make the prospects for exporting industrial goods more attractive and, consequently, should stimulate greater investment in the productive capacity of export items. Whether or not this hoped-for industrialisation will be realised is at yet uncertain, as it takes time for these incentives to be translated first into action and second into observable results.

In the final analysis, the G.S.P. should be judged by the effectiveness of the incentives created by the preferential tariffs to contribute to expanded developing-country exports of manufactured goods. After all, the G.S.P. does provide for preferential duty-free tariffs for the vast majority of industrial products imported by the donors. The crucial question is: Does the dismal picture indicated by the data derive from an unwillingness on the part of the donor countries to allow the objectives of the G.S.P. to be fulfilled? Or does it derive from the fact that the current trade pattern of the developing countries happens to be inopportune? If it is due to the nature of existing trade patterns, then the G.S.P. may be appropriate for stimulating a change in the composition of beneficiary exports to the donor countries. On the other hand, if it is due to the nature of the preference schemes, then we can anticipate that the incentives created by the G.S.P. will fail to bring about the desired increase in beneficiary exports of manufactured products.

The evidence gleaned from this examination of trade flows indicates that both elements are in fact important. Over one-half of beneficiary exports enter duty-free under M.F.N. tariffs – hence the picture is to a large extent due to an inopportune trade pattern. But three-quarters of what is left is *excluded* from preferential treatment, either to protect domestic producers of import-sensitive industrial products, or because it simply involves agricultural and fishery products.

In summary, the G.S.P. as it operates in the mid-1970s provides a wide scope for the developing countries to export manufactured products which they currently do not export; but the bulk of those products which they do export, and therefore in which they have a demonstrated international comparative advantage, are excluded from the G.S.P. The G.S.P. incentives thus tell the developing countries to stop doing what they do well and instead start doing something else. Does it make sense from a world-wide efficiency standpoint for the developing countries, with their abundant labour supplies, to curtail their production of labour-intensive textiles, leather products, and the like? And are they to increase their production of, say, computers, jet aircraft and such other products simply because they are covered by the G.S.P.?

It seems equally illogical from the capital-abundant donor-country standpoint. Why do these countries insist on protecting their labour-intensive sectors? Why not reallocate productive factors into activities having higher labour-productivity? Apparently even these countries have pools of relatively unskilled labour that are currently unsuited for employment in high-technology capital-intensive industries. Thus it is economically desirable to have some labour-intensive employment opportunities. There is little doubt that the most advanced industrial countries will continue to have productive activity all across the product spectrum – from the most sophisticated to the least. And when you combine this 'fact of life' with political pressures, much of which is simply for the *status quo*, it is not difficult to see why the G.S.P. is what it is.

To carry this line of reasoning one more step, if the donor countries are determined to protect these employment opportunities for their unskilled, the developing countries should best realise the consequences. They cannot count on textile exports to provide a rapid increase in export earnings. Thus they should limit their investment in these sectors to a level sufficient to satisfy local markets and maintain (not expand) their share of world markets; and they must concentrate new investment in those sectors where world markets are open and expanding, while at the same time guarding against over-committing investment resources to a single sector – today's open world market may be closed tomorrow. If this type of scenario proves to be the story of tomorrow's structure of world trade, the G.S.P. product coverage, as it now stands, may provide a desirable mix of incentives away from sectors in which world markets will not be allowed to grow rapidly and into sectors in which future world market shares are currently up for grabs. But for who?

MAJOR DEVELOPING-COUNTRY SUPPLIERS

The goal of the G.S.P. is to help all developing countries help themselves – through trade rather than aid. Consequently, the benefits of this programme will accrue to the developing countries according to their ability to export products covered by the G.S.P. schemes. Obviously, there is a great diversity in the abilities of the developing countries to export manufactures. The data contained in Table 4.3 demonstrate this point. The concentration of G.S.P. trade is tremendous. Based on 1970 trade flows of products covered by the various G.S.P. schemes, nine developing countries (including the territory of Hong Kong) account for over 70 per cent of G.S.P. trade; and there are over

TABLE 4.3

Estimated 1970 G.S.P. imports of industrial products
*from major beneficiary suppliers**

Beneficiary supplier	G.S.P. imports	
	Value ($ million)	Share of total (per cent)
Taiwan†	565	16
Mexico	432	12
Yugoslavia	399	11
South Korea	329	9
Hong Kong‡	254	7
Brazil	190	5
Singapore	168	5
India	144	4
Iran	104	3
Sub-total	2585	72
Other beneficiaries¶	1035	28
Total	3620	100

* Only major donor trade (the United States, the E.E.C. and Japan) are included. The figures for the United States were estimated from 1973 trade flows and deflated to 1970 levels; figures for the E.E.C. were estimated from 1972 data. The actual product list for the United States was not available when these data were compiled; instead the President's provisional list was used. The major product deletions involve import-sensitive electronic items; but numerous other import-sensitive items were deleted as well. The U.S. G.S.P. trade flows were cut roughly in half; the new 'total' figures should be reduced from $3620 million to $2736 million.
† Japan's G.S.P. imports from Taiwan were estimated since Taiwan cannot be mentioned individually in any U.N. document. The remainder of Taiwan's estimated G.S.P. trade is accounted for by the United States since Taiwan is not a beneficiary of the E.E.C. G.S.P.
‡ The figure for Hong Kong does not include the United States or Japan. Hong Kong's beneficiary status under the U.S. G.S.P. was unknown at the time these data were compiled. Japan has recently added Hong Kong to its beneficiary list; however, there is a special list of products for which Hong Kong exports *do not* receive G.S.P. tariff treatment.
¶ The most significant 'minor suppliers' are Zambia ($270 million in exports, copper), Chile ($110 million, mostly copper), the Philippines ($67 million), Argentina ($64 million), Peru ($60 million) and Malaysia ($50 million).
SOURCE: UNCTAD Secretariat calculations reported in documents *TD/B/C.5/15*, *TD/B/C.5/34* and *TD/B/C.5/38*.

110 beneficiary developing countries not counting the forty or so beneficiary territories. In fact, four countries – Taiwan, Mexico, Yugoslavia and South Korea – account for just under one-half of all G.S.P. trade.

The export potential of these major suppliers was responsible for a number of problems during the initial setting-up of the G.S.P. as well as during the negotiations for improving the G.S.P. schemes. From the outset the G.S.P. was envisaged to be a non-discriminatory system in favour of all developing countries. But the only trade policy which could immediately help the poorest developing countries must be based on extremely low-technology products such as textiles, leather products, and so on. The donors feared that including such products would cause havoc in their domestic markets due to the major suppliers. In essence, the agreement to have a non-discriminatory programme prevented the donors from including the only products that would enable the least developed countries to benefit from the G.S.P. The search for products which would benefit the poorest led to the unfortunate but not unexpected realisation that the poorest countries are minor suppliers of even those products that account for the bulk of their own export earnings. Certainly, little could be done to share the benefits of the G.S.P. on a fair basis.

On the other hand, if the G.S.P. were a programme limited to the fifty or so poorest developing countries and territories, the product coverage could be exceedingly broad with little danger to donor-country producers of import-competing products. Under this circumstance the G.S.P. could be what it was envisaged to be – a non-discriminatory (for the fifty) duty-free programme covering all manufactures and semi-manufactures, including processed and semi-processed agricultural and fishery products. But as more advanced developing countries (defined in terms of export potential rather than *per capita* income) are added to the beneficiary lists, the potential for serious import-displacement in the donor markets increases and, consequently, the more limited will be the product coverage. Thus there is a very definite trade-off between a broad product coverage and the principle of non-discrimination being applied to all developing countries. If the G.S.P. permitted the donors to discriminate against G.S.P. trade from certain developing countries, the product coverage would in all likelihood be much broader.

But the G.S.P. negotiations accepted a very strong nondiscriminatory self-election concept that resulted in very broad beneficiary lists; and, as was just demonstrated, this led to very uneven benefits accruing to particular developing countries. As a result, the donors searched for some mechanism that would more equitably share the benefits of the G.S.P. among a much wider range of developing countries without violating this non-discrimination principle. In the end the major donors – the E.E.C., Japan and the United States – each adopted ceiling limitations on trade which would receive G.S.P. tariff treatment. Under the three systems, whenever any beneficiary country's exports of a particular product exceeded a predetermined limit, M.F.N. tariff rates would be applied rather than G.S.P. rates. These ceiling limits – applied on a non-discriminatory basis of course – affect the G.S.P. trade of only a few major exporting beneficiary countries. Thus the principle of non-discrimination is honoured while at the same time the G.S.P. donors could treat imports from various sources differently depending upon the volume of trade involved.

These ceiling systems provided a second benefit for the donors. When the G.S.P. was negotiated, the principle of non-reciprocity in favour of the developing countries came at a price; the donors would incorporate safeguard measures in their G.S.P. schemes to protect domestic producers in the event that G.S.P. trade increased sufficiently to disrupt domestic markets. Most donors simply resorted to a GATT-type escape clause; but, as just mentioned, the major donors imposed limits on the annual trade flows that would be granted G.S.P. tariff treatment. These safeguards and their consequences are the subject of the next chapter.

5
Safeguard Measures

In introducing its preference schemes each donor country reserves the right to withdraw or modify G.S.P. tariff treatment; and such limitations could be applied against a given beneficiary country for one or more products or against a given product for one or more beneficiaries. Thus the donor-country reservation was extremely broad in its potential application.

The rationale underlying this limitation was twofold. First, since the G.S.P. was negotiated on a non-reciprocal basis, the donors considered G.S.P. tariff treatment to be a unilateral concession. Anything which is unilaterally given can thereby be unilaterally taken away. But of course the beneficiaries did not consider the G.S.P. to be a gift; instead they rationalised it as a justified modification in the rules governing international trade whereby unequal trading partners should be treated unequally. The developing countries argued that they deserved preferential tariff treatment as compensation for their producers' disadvantaged position in world markets.

This latter rationalisation was more widely accepted by both donors and beneficiaries. If G.S.P. tariff treatment is important to the developing countries, exports of certain products to donor country markets will increase significantly. In some cases local firms and workers may be unable to fully adjust to this new G.S.P.-stimulated import competition. In anticipation of such situations it was agreed that the G.S.P. schemes incorporate so-called 'safeguard measures' to protect donor-country markets from undue disruption.

The safeguard measures contained in the various G.S.P. schemes take a number of forms – some are very explicit while others are more subtle. The most direct form of safeguard is to prevent G.S.P.-caused market disruption before it can occur, i.e. exclude products in which the beneficiaries are likely to have an immediate export capability, such as textiles and leather goods. All donors, in one form or another, have invoked this type of safeguard. A more subtle variant of this safeguard is to establish G.S.P. tariff rates which are minimally below normal M.F.N. duties. As an example, for agricultural and fishery products, the E.E.C. initially granted G.S.P. duties averaging 4 percentage points below M.F.N. tariffs. These implicit safeguards, though important in their own right, will not be discussed further in this chapter – the results of their invocation was the subject of the previous chapter.

The explicit safeguards take two basic forms. The first provides that G.S.P. tariff treatment should cease whenever a causal tie can be established between an increase in G.S.P. trade and economic injury to donor-country firms or workers. This is the traditional escape-clause measure as embodied in GATT, and contained in every U.S. tariff negotiation law enacted since 1951. Such a GATT-type escape clause is contained in every G.S.P. scheme.

In theory the escape clause is a relatively equitable arrangement; expanded G.S.P. imports are permitted until there is a demonstrated relationship between such imports and domestic injury. However, in practice there are serious problems because of the time lag between initial injury and the implementation of corrective measures. In the meantime the injury to domestic firms and workers may be irreparable. There needs to be an effective anticipatory escape clause established whereby the rate of growth of imports could be moderated to provide time for inefficient domestic import-competing factors of production to be reallocated to other productive activities, but unfortunately there is no effective anticipatory system at present. In this void a second type of safeguard measure has also been proposed, namely placing limits on the volume of trade which will be granted G.S.P. tariff treatment. Generally these 'ceiling' limits are administered by product group, with the groups being defined more or less narrowly depending upon the proven ability of developing countries to export particular products.

In practice the escape-clause safeguards have posed no problems for G.S.P. trade. Such a clause has been invoked in only one case – the United Kingdom ceased G.S.P. tariff treatment on imports of leather from Argentina, Brazil, Colombia and Uruguay prior to the enlargement of the E.E.C. Currently no escape clause is in force against G.S.P. trade. On the other hand, the systems of ceilings introduced by the E.E.C. and Japan have proven extremely troublesome. In the recently introduced U.S. scheme two new types of G.S.P. trade-limiting measures have been introduced – a set of 'competitive need' criteria and a non-causal import-relief measure. The ceiling systems of the E.E.C. and Japan and the new measures introduced by the United States will be discussed in turn.

CEILING SYSTEMS OF THE E.E.C. AND JAPAN

The E.E.C. and Japan protect their domestic producers from potential injury through systems of ceilings, a method which at first glance appears quite reasonable. G.S.P. tariff treatment will apply on imports up to a ceiling; M.F.N. duties are charged on imports in excess of the ceiling. Thus the ceiling does not limit imports but simply determines the tariff rate to be applied. This seems like a justifiable safeguard in that domestic producers are ultimately protected only when preferential imports from developing countries grow too rapidly, i.e. when G.S.P. imports exceed the ceiling. In the final analysis, however, the reasonableness of these systems depends upon the levels of the ceilings.

Since the ceilings are designed for the purpose of protecting domestic producers and since the international competitiveness of these producers differs from industry to industry, the ceiling systems of both the E.E.C. and Japan are administered on a product-by-product basis. Imports from developing countries are classified into product categories with a separate ceiling established for each category – the E.E.C. defines approximately 800 individual items whereas Japan specifies some 200.* Also, since the goods have been divided into a number of product groups, it is possible that G.S.P. tariff treatment will apply on some goods – whose product-group ceiling has not been exhausted – and M.F.N. tariffs will apply on other goods – whose ceilings have not been exhausted.

The ceiling level for each product is normally assigned on the basis of the following formula: the sum of (1) donor imports of the product from all beneficiaries during a base year and (2) a growth factor related to the level of E.E.C. imports of the product from all non-beneficiary countries.† The term 'normally' is no accident as the E.E.C. has departed from the formula in particular instances. For example, no growth factors were provided for a number of 'sensitive' textile and petroleum products. For a few articles, for example chinaware, the growth factor was reduced to 1 per cent of non-beneficiary trade. The ceilings for plywood and veneer were also manipulated to protect the interests of the African Associates. Japan, however, religiously applies the formula. In some cases the resulting ceilings are ridiculous. For example, when Japan did not import a product from any source during 1968 or 1969, the ceiling formula yields a 'zero' ceiling. This situation occurred for nine product groups. A tenth 'zero' ceiling occurred for copper due to a peculiarity in Japan's 'sliding' M.F.N. duty. The duty on copper depends upon the world price of copper and ranges from duty-free (when the world price is high) to roughly 7 per cent *ad valorem* (when the world price is low). During 1968 and 1969 the world price of copper was high; thus copper was admitted to Japan duty-free. Since no dutiable copper was imported into Japan the initial ceiling was 'zero'.

The reasonableness of the ceilings depend ultimately on the growth factor. If developing countries are already major suppliers of a product, they have demonstrated an ability to compete in world markets on an M.F.N. basis and, consequently, do not need preferential treatment. Moreover, it is in precisely these cases that special G.S.P. tariff treatment is most likely to cause injury to domestic producers. Thus a small growth factor, which

---

* The product-category definitions are taken from the donor-country tariff schedules, for example the E.E.C. defines products at the four-digit Brussels Tariff Nomenclature (B.T.N.) level.

† The ceilings are defined only for industrial products; an escape clause is relied on to protect producers of agricultural and fishery items. When the G.S.P. was first introduced in 1971, the E.E.C. chose 1968 as the base year for both parts of the ceiling formula; Japan chose 1968 for the first part and 1969 for the second.

means that any significant increase in developing-country trade will face normal M.F.N. tariffs, is not unreasonable. It is in situations such as these that the ceiling formula yields a small growth factor since non-beneficiaries will be relatively minor suppliers. On the other hand, for those products in which the developing countries are non-competitive and therefore account for only a minor share of trade, a growth factor based on third-country trade will provide large ceilings. In these instances the expected increase in beneficiary trade should pose no problem to domestic producers as there is substantial opportunity for G.S.P. trade to simply displace imports from non-beneficiary sources. Conceptually this ceiling formula is quite reasonable and well suited to provide developing-country suppliers improved access to E.E.C. and Japanese markets without causing excessive injury to domestic producers. It is only when the formula is examined more closely that shortcomings appear.

The first problem in applying any ceiling formula is one of a time lag. Since ceiling limits are produced prior to the beginning of the year for which they are to apply, the actual trade flows used in the calculations must predate the ceiling year by at least two years. For example, ceilings to apply for calendar year 1977 are published in December of 1976. Obviously trade data covering the entire 1976 year are not available; thus data for 1975 are used. When the E.E.C. first introduced its scheme in July 1971, ceilings were calculated from 1968 trade data using the following formula:*

$$Q_{71} = m_{68} + 0.05(M_{68} - m_{68}),$$

where Q_{71} is the ceiling for a given product group to apply in 1971, m_{68} is the 1968 level of E.E.C. imports from beneficiary countries;† and M_{68} is the 1968 level of E.E.C. imports from the rest of the world. The first term on the right-hand side is called the basic ceiling, with the second being the growth factor, i.e. 5 per cent of E.E.C. imports come from non-beneficiaries. The basic ceiling remains fixed while the growth factor is recalculated each year using more recent data, but which still lags the year for which the ceilings apply by three years. Thus the total ceilings will increase from year to year by 5 per cent of the growth in E.E.C. imports from non-beneficiaries (which occurred three years earlier).‡ The problem with this formula is that imports

---

* The formula for Japan differs in two respects: first, the growth factor is 10 per cent rather than 5 per cent of Japanese imports from non-beneficiaries; and second, 1969 data were initially used to calculate the growth factor. The second term on the right-hand side is thus $0.10(M_{69} - m_{69})$.

† Since the African countries associated with the E.E.C. have more favourable tariff treatment under the association agreements, E.E.C. imports from these countries are not counted with beneficiary trade in calculating the ceilings but rather with non-beneficiaries to increase the growth factor. Similarly G.S.P. imports from these countries are not counted towards the filling of ceilings.

‡ Under Japan's system the increases in ceilings would be *10* per cent of the growth in Japanese imports from non-beneficiaries (which occurred *two* years earlier).

of many products from the beneficiaries grew quite rapidly during recent years, resulting in 1971 imports exceeding the 1971 ceiling. In such cases the ceilings might be called 'closed-ended', meaning that the G.S.P. tariff rates apply only on a trade volume that would have occurred even in the absence of any G.S.P. tariff incentives. Any increase in imports from the beneficiaries would face M.F.N. duties; consequently, the G.S.P. will not contribute to any increase in developing-country trade.

The benefits which the developing countries are to receive from the G.S.P. depend upon the price incentive created by the preferential tariff margins. The effect of this ceiling formula on the price incentive can be demonstrated using Figure 5.1. Let DD represent the donor demand for imports of a

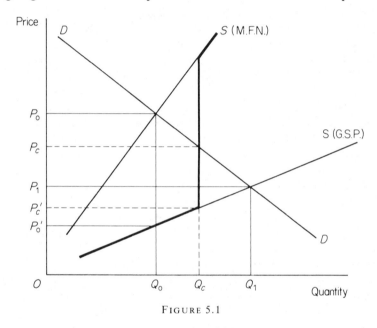

FIGURE 5.1

particular product from beneficiary developing countries, S(G.S.P.) the duty-free beneficiary export supply curve, and S(M.F.N.) the tariff-ridden beneficiary export supply curve. The pre-G.S.P. level of trade is OQ_0, with OP_0 the price paid by donor importers; $P_0 P_0'$ is the M.F.N. tariff rate (which is equal to the G.S.P. tariff margin) yielding export earnings to the developing countries of OP_0' times OQ_0. When duty-free G.S.P. tariff treatment is implemented, the level of trade increases to OQ_1, as donor importers shift to the lower-priced beneficiary suppliers. The benefits to developing countries can be measured in export earnings, which increase to OP_1 times OQ_1. This would be the case if no limitations applied to G.S.P. trade. However, the existence of ceilings changes the story. Let OQ_c be the level of imports on which G.S.P. tariffs will apply; imports in excess of OQ_c will be charged

M.F.N. duties. Thus the beneficiary export supply curve becomes discontinuous at Q_c; it coincides with S(G.S.P.) for a trade flow less than OQ_c, and with S(M.F.N.) for a trade flow in excess of OQ_c – the new beneficiary export supply curve is depicted by the heavy line. If Q_c lies to the right of Q_1, the ceiling is 'open-ended' and ineffective – the G.S.P. price incentives operate to their fullest extent. But if Q_c lies to the left of Q_1 as shown, the post-G.S.P. level of trade expands only to Q_c. The equilibrium price is indeterminant (between OP'_c and OP_c) and depends upon the relative bargaining strength of beneficiary exporters versus donor importers. But in any case beneficiary export earnings increase from OP'_0 times OQ_0 to at least OP'_c times OQ_c, and possibly more.

However, if Q_c lies to the left of Q_0, the beneficiary export supply curve is discontinuous to the left of Q_0 and therefore coincides with S(M.F.N.), where it intersects DD. In this case the post-G.S.P. level of trade is unchanged at OQ_0 – no trade expansion occurs. There is the question of tariff revenue forgone by the donor on the ceiling level of trade which amounts to $P_0 P'_0$ times OQ_c – the gain to beneficiary exporters depends on their market power relative to that of donor importers. But whatever 'tariff revenue' accrues to beneficiary exporters would, in reality, constitute an 'aid' transfer rather than a 'trade' benefit since no G.S.P. price incentives operate *to expand* the level of beneficiary exports to the E.E.C. or Japan.

The major question in evaluating the impact of the ceilings is whether the ceilings are exceeded by that level of imports which would have occurred in the absence of the G.S.P. To illustrate, consider the following hypothetical example. Let 1968 E.E.C. imports of a particular product be $100 with beneficiary countries supplying $25, i.e. the beneficiaries initially account for 25 per cent of the E.E.C. import market. Further, assume that normal E.E.C. imports from all sources grew 10 per cent annually. Thus by 1971, the year in which the E.E.C. introduced its G.S.P. scheme, E.E.C. imports from beneficiaries would be $33·28. Using the ceiling formula, we find the ceiling level of imports to be $28·75 [$25 + 0·05(100 − 25)]. The ceiling (OQ_c) is less than the level of E.E.C. imports that would have occurred in the absence of the G.S.P. (OQ_0), i.e. the ceiling is 'closed-ended'. Of course this is only a hypothetical case and cannot be expected to hold for each and every product covered by the E.E.C. or Japanese schemes; but at the same time it is not so extreme that it will never happen. This example illustrates the very real possibility that the ceiling systems will render the G.S.P. ineffective from the start for some products. But what about the others?

Consider a second example in which the initial beneficiary share of E.E.C. imports is only 10 per cent. By 1971 the normal level of E.E.C. imports from the beneficiaries, assuming the same 10 per cent growth rate, would be $13·31 and the ceiling $14·50; the ceiling is 'open-ended'. However, over time beneficiary exports would continue to grow, yielding normal non-G.S.P. trade flows of $14·64 for 1972 and $16·11 for 1973. The ceiling levels for these subsequent years would also grow due to the annual recalculation of the ceiling growth factor. For 1972 the ceiling would be $10 plus 5 per cent of 1969 E.E.C. imports from non-beneficiaries, or $14·95 [$10 + 0·05 ($110 − $11)]; by 1973 the ceiling would increase to $15·45. Upon comparing the ceilings with the normal beneficiary trade flows over time, we see that the ceiling which is 'open-ended' in 1971 remains 'open-ended' during 1972 but becomes 'closed-ended' by 1973.

A number of similar calculations were made to illustrate this ceiling concept for different initial beneficiary market shares and different beneficiary export growth rates (non-beneficiary trade with the E.E.C. was assumed to grow at the empirical rate of 10 per cent annually). The results of these calculations, which report the first year in which the ceiling becomes 'closed-ended', are presented in Table 5.1. A casual examination of these calcula-

TABLE 5.1

The first year in which the E.E.C. ceiling becomes closed-ended*

Beneficiary growth rates† (per cent)	Beneficiary share of E.E.C. import market (per cent)									
	1	2	3	4	5	7½	10	15	20	25
5	O	O	O	O	O	O	O	1976	1973	C
10	O	O	O	O	O	1975	1973	C	C	C
15	O	O	1979	1976	1974	1972	C	C	C	C
20	O	1978	1975	1973	1972	C	C	C	C	C
25	1979	1975	1973	1973	C	C	C	C	C	C

Symbols: O – the ceiling remains 'open-ended' after ten years, the initially anticipated life of the G.S.P.; C – the ceiling is 'closed-ended' during the first year (1971) of the G.S.P.

* Similar calculations for Japan show the ceilings to become 'closed-ended' about five years later. However, a continuation of recent trade patterns and growth rates will result in the 'average' ceiling becoming 'closed-ended' during 1974.

† E.E.C. imports from non-beneficiaries are assumed to grow at the rate of 10 per cent annually, which is the actual rate observed during the 1960s.

tions indicates that the ceilings are likely to remain 'open-ended' only when the share or growth rate of E.E.C. imports from beneficiaries is quite low. However, during the 1967–70 period E.E.C. imports from beneficiaries of products covered by the scheme grew 20 per cent annually. Hence the ceilings are likely to prove inadequate much before the end of the anticipated ten-year life of the G.S.P.; and when the ceilings become 'closed-ended' the G.S.P. ceases being a 'trade' policy. Although valid, this conclusion only holds 'on the average'. Certainly some products will fall outside the range of this conclusion. Unfortunately, however, it is likely to hold for the vast majority of products in which the developing countries have demonstrated an export capability.

Another element in determining the restrictiveness of the ceilings involves the level of aggregation used in defining product groups. For example, if those products in which beneficiary countries have demonstrated an ability to export are defined narrowly, beneficiaries will be major suppliers and, hence, the growth factor will be a small part of the over-all ceiling. It is likely that such products will have 'closed-ended' ceilings. And if products which developing countries do not export – computers, aircraft, heavy machinery, and so on – are defined broadly, the growth factor will be large, providing huge 'open-ended' ceilings. But few developing countries will be able to take advantage of the G.S.P. for these products. Japan has exploited this opportunity for restricting G.S.P. trade. Roughly one-third of Japan's aggregate ceiling volume of trade involves six products – machinery and electrical equipment, hydrocarbon chemicals, precision instruments, aircraft and parts, computers and components, miscellaneous chemical products; beneficiary exports of these six products amount to less than 2 per cent of their G.S.P. trade with Japan.

The final proof of the inadequacy of the ceilings must await a product-by-product comparison of donor imports from beneficiaries with the ceiling levels. Such a comparison is presented in Chapter 7.

Up to this point I have concentrated on the inadequacy of the over-all level of ceilings which limit G.S.P. imports from all beneficiaries combined. However, the ceiling systems of the E.E.C. and Japan contain additional limitations on G.S.P. trade which apply to individual beneficiary countries. The E.E.C. scheme also has a provision which allocates the ceilings for some products among the individual member states. The first of these complications is commonly referred to as the 'maximum-amount' limitation and the second as the 'allocation' limitation; these concepts will be treated in turn.

The maximum-amount limitation

The maximum-amount provision limits G.S.P. imports from a single beneficiary to 50 per cent of the ceiling for each product group; M.F.N. tariffs will apply on imports in excess of the 50 per cent amount for the affected beneficiary.* However, other beneficiaries can continue to export the same product under G.S.P. tariff treatment. The rationale for this maximum-amount provision is to limit the preferences granted to the more competitive beneficiary countries and thereby reserve a substantial share of the ceilings for the less competitive developing countries. The effect, however, is to make the G.S.P. more restrictive toward the major suppliers, with minimal benefits for the others.

To illustrate, suppose that a given product has a ceiling of $100,000 and that beneficiary exports will be $120,000 – $80,000 originating in one country and the remaining $40,000 spread over the other beneficiary coun-

* The E.E.C. designates maximum-amount limits of 20 per cent or 30 per cent for a number of 'sensitive' products.

tries. Without the maximum-amount limit, $20,000 in trade ($120,000 trade less $100,000 ceiling) would face M.F.N. duties; this trade could have originated in the major supplier or any of the minor suppliers. But at the worst, $20,000 in beneficiary trade would be denied G.S.P. tariff treatment. But with the maximum-amount limitation imports from the major supplier in excess of the 50 per cent limit would be denied G.S.P. treatment – in this case $30,000 ($80,000 less $50,000). As a result G.S.P. trade from all beneficiaries would be reduced to $90,000 ($50,000 from the major supplier and $40,000 from the others). Since this trade flow is less than the $100,000 ceiling, G.S.P. tariff treatment would apply on all trade from the minor beneficiary suppliers. However, the major supplier would be denied G.S.P. tariff treatment on $30,000, whereas without the maximum-amount limit he would be denied G.S.P. tariffs on, at most, $20,000 in trade. The major supplier is worse off with this limit. On the other hand, the minor suppliers cannot lose – without the maximum-amount limit they risk losing G.S.P. tariff treatment on up to $20,000 in trade; with the limit they are assured (in this example) of G.S.P. treatment on all of their exports. Thus in the first instance this maximum-amount limit seems reasonable and in line with its 'benefit-sharing' objective.

But before judging the maximum-amount limit, consider the following alternative example. Suppose total trade of the product, having a $100,000 ceiling, is only $90,000, with $80,000 originating in the major beneficiary country. Since total beneficiary trade is less than the ceiling, all should receive G.S.P. tariff treatment. However, the 50 per cent maximum-amount rule limits the major beneficiary G.S.P. trade to $50,000; $30,000 in trade is denied G.S.P. tariff treatment. And for what reason? To reserve a portion of the ceiling for minor beneficiary suppliers. In this case the maximum-amount limitation has simply reduced the total benefits of the G.S.P. without benefiting a single developing country since the minor beneficiaries are unable to fill the portion of the ceilings reserved for them. This latter example corresponds quite well to the actual situation for a number of important products.

The normal criticism of this limitation imposed by the E.E.C. and Japan is that – as in any system involving quotas within quotas – it is likely to result in a wasteful non-utilisation of a significant portion of the already inadequate ceilings. If the purpose of the G.S.P. is to expand developing-country exports, it is important that the G.S.P. provides price incentives which operate at the margin. The ceiling and maximum-amount limitations must be large enough for expanded levels of trade to receive G.S.P. tariff treatment. The problem with the ceiling and maximum-amount limitations is that they often prevent the price incentive from operating on *expanded* levels of trade. This conclusion holds for the G.S.P. schemes of both the E.E.C. and Japan, but the E.E.C. goes one better than Japan by sub-dividing its ceilings for some products into member-state allocations.

The E.E.C. ceiling allocation limitation

For the administration of its system of ceilings the E.E.C. divides industrial products into two groups: goods whose markets are expected to be adversely effected by G.S.P. imports from developing countries have been designated as 'sensitive' products; other products are designated 'non-sensitive'. G.S.P. trade in non-sensitive products is subject only to the ceiling and maximum-amount limitations, as discussed above. The sensitive products face these limitations,* but in addition each ceiling is sub-divided among the E.E.C. member states into seven separate member-state ceilings – called 'tariff quotas'. In this regard the European Community ceases to exist; instead there are seven independent states each having a prespecified share of the total ceiling. The share breakdown among the member states is based on an arbitrary 'burden-sharing' concept which has little relationship to the share composition of actual E.E.C. trade with the developing countries. Rather the E.E.C. ceiling is sub-divided according to fixed shares based on general economic criteria, relating to external trade, gross national product and population. The fixed shares applying to all products are as follows: Benelux 10·5 per cent, Denmark 5 per cent, France 19 per cent, West Germany 27·5 per cent, Ireland 1 per cent, Italy 15 per cent, and the United Kingdom 22 per cent. In the event that G.S.P. imports of a sensitive product exceed a member-state allocation (say, for France) additional imports into France from any beneficiary source will be charged M.F.N. duties. However, if these same goods were to be imported into another E.E.C. member state instead, G.S.P. tariffs would apply.

The problem with this allocation is twofold. First, the formula is not consistent with the actual division of E.E.C. imports of G.S.P. products from the beneficiaries. For example, when the Community of Six first introduced its G.S.P. scheme in 1971, the allocation shares were as follows: Benelux 15·5 per cent, France 27·1 per cent, West Germany 37·5 per cent, and Italy 20·3 per cent. In comparison, based on 1969 data, the shares of E.E.C. member-state imports of sensitive products from beneficiaries were as follows: Benelux 19·7 per cent, France 7·9 per cent, West Germany 55·4 per cent, and Italy 17 per cent. The mismatching is obvious: the French ceiling allocation is 27·1 per cent compared with an actual trade share of only 7·9 per cent, which contrasts with West Germany's 37·5 per cent ceiling and 55·4 per cent trade share. The second problem is that the ceiling shares are the same for every product. Obviously, actual E.E.C. imports are not invariantly divided among the member states for every product.

The significance of this limitation based on fixed shares is illustrated in Table 5.2. For bicycle trade, the Benelux allocation falls short of Benelux's

---

* As mentioned above, the maximum-amount limits for sensitive products are often less than 50 per cent of the ceiling – generally 20 or 30 per cent.

actual share of E.E.C. imports by over 48 per cent of the total. Thus only 52 per cent of E.E.C. imports will receive G.S.P. tariff treatment. In the case of glassware West Germany has a 46 per cent shortfall; only 54 per cent of E.E.C. imports will benefit from G.S.P. In total, both Benelux and West Germany are seriously under-allocated, such that approximately 20 percent of E.E.C. imports from all beneficiaries will face M.F.N. duties.

In summary, the ceiling systems of both the E.E.C. and Japan involve ceiling limits on G.S.P. imports from all beneficiaries combined and maximum-amount limits on G.S.P. imports from individual beneficiaries. In addition, the E.E.C. sub-divides industrial product groups into two classes – sensitive and non-sensitive; the sensitive product ceilings are then allocated among the member states according to a fixed formula. These systems sterilise the

TABLE 5.2

E.E.C. allocation rule versus actual trade patterns (per cent)

E.E.C. member state	Allocation rule	Bicycles		Glassware		All sensitive	
		1969 trade	G.S.P. trade	1969 trade	G.S.P. trade	1969 trade	G.S.P. trade
Benelux	15·5	63·4	15·1*	6·6	6·6	19·7	15·1*
France	27·1	13·6	13·6	7·7	7·7	7·9	7·9
West Germany	37·5	23·0	23·0	83·2	37·5*	55·4	37·5*
Italy	20·3	0·0	0·0	2·5	2·5	17·0	20·3
Total	100·0	100·0	51·7	100·0	54·3	100·0	80·8

* The remaining trade is charged M.F.N. tariffs as it exceeds the maximum member-state allocation for G.S.P. tariff treatment.
SOURCE: UNCTAD Secretariat calculations as reported in document *TD/B/C.5/15*, pp. 126, 151.

trade-expanding incentives of the G.S.P. since, in many cases, the ceilings are so restrictive that expanded trade will face M.F.N. rather than G.S.P. tariffs. Further, it was shown that the maximum-amount limit can lead to the sterilisation of G.S.P. trade for major suppliers even in cases where the over-all ceiling is not exhausted. And finally, the allocation rule of the E.E.C. could sterilise the trade-expanding incentives of the G.S.P. even when the total ceiling is not exhausted and the maximum-amount limit is not constrained.

In addition to these so-called price-incentive sterilising properties, the ceiling systems also hinder G.S.P. trade as they introduce an element of uncertainty. G.S.P. trade in many products will be affected by one or more of the ceiling limits, and hence neither the importer nor the exporter will know in advance whether G.S.P. tariffs will apply when their goods are cleared through customs. International trade involves contracting at one date for goods which will be received by the importer at a later date with the time lag normally measured in weeks and months. Consequently, it is quite conceivable that a shipment could be ordered at a time when G.S.P. tariffs would apply, but by the time the goods arrived for customs clearance the ceiling could be exhausted (or a maximum-amount or ceiling-allocation limit could apply). In order to analyse the implications of this uncertainty, we must understand the techniques used by the E.E.C. and Japan in administering trade under the G.S.P. regulations.

E.E.C. ADMINISTRATION OF G.S.P. TRADE

Recall that the E.E.C. has defined two broad categories of products – sensitive and non-sensitive. As might be expected the administration of G.S.P. trade in sensitive products is much tighter than for non-sensitive products. Trade in non-sensitive items is administered at the Community level with the geographical distribution of E.E.C. imports among the member states being irrelevant in determining whether G.S.P. tariff rates will apply. The only requirement is that the ceiling or maximum-amount limits at the Community level have not been exceeded for the particular product.

Since G.S.P. trade in these products is not considered to pose a serious threat to domestic producers, the product groups have not been precisely defined. Imports from the beneficiaries are admitted on a first-come first-served basis and are not closely monitored by the E.E.C. It is quite possible that G.S.P. imports could exceed a ceiling or maximum-amount limit without the cessation of G.S.P. tariff treatment. In practice, the re-establishment of a particular M.F.N. tariff rate is the result of action that is originally initiated by a domestic producer of an import-competing product. The domestic producer complains to the appropriate national authority, who formally brings the issue before the E.E.C. Commission. The Commission, upon receipt of the complaint, calculates the ceiling and maximum-amount limits for the product in question and compares these limits with the year's actual G.S.P. imports which have been periodically communicated to the Commission by all member states. If one of the limits has been exceeded, appropriate action is taken to re-establish M.F.N. duties on further imports from one or more beneficiaries, as the case may dictate.

This method of administration presents two special problems. The first deals with the lack of *a priori* product definition. Since the complaint is initiated at the local level, the producer can define the product that is adversely affecting his market position. The only question for him is to 'properly' define the product so that a ceiling or maximum-amount limit is exceeded. Since each member state has access to all information concerning G.S.P. trade, the claimant need only calculate ceilings and maximum amounts for the product defined at several different levels of aggregation and then compare these different limits with actual G.S.P. trade. The claim submitted to the Commission will then embody that specific product definition for which the ceiling or maximum-amount limit is in fact exceeded. The outcome is then certain. In general, narrowly defined product groups are more likely to have restrictive ceilings. Consequently, if the member state calculates actual G.S.P. trade to be close to a ceiling limit, the complaint will narrowly define the product. But if the limit is grossly exceeded, a broader product definition may be submitted to protect producers of closely related though somewhat different products.

The second problem is that importers cannot know on the date when they contract for imports from beneficiaries that the goods will receive G.S.P. tariff treatment when cleared through customs. Depending upon the contract price it is possible that a change of tariff status (from G.S.P. to M.F.N.) could turn a profitable import contract into a loss. As a hedge against such a possibility importers are likely to contract for G.S.P. imports only at prices that would be profitable even if M.F.N. duties were to be charged. If the imports do gain G.S.P. tariff treatment, so much the better as they receive a windfall profit. But beneficiary exporters should not expect to receive bids which reflect G.S.P. tariff rates since it is unlikely that E.E.C. importers will be willing to accept the risk of M.F.N. duties applying. About the only benefit that beneficiary exporters can expect to receive is a slightly increased volume of trade at normal prices (as if the G.S.P. did not exist) due to the inducement of possible importer windfall profits. As experience is gained with G.S.P. trading, this conclusion may be modified in favour of beneficiary exporters of those products which have historically gained G.S.P. tariff treatment.

Nowhere in the E.E.C. regulations governing G.S.P. trade is there mention of any products being designated as 'semi-sensitive'. There is, however, a list of semi-sensitive items within the category of non-sensitive products. The major importance of this distinction is that imports of these semi-sensitive items are subject to special surveillance. Ceiling and maximum-amount limits have been precalculated to facilitate the rapid re-establishment of M.F.N. duties once a limit has been exceeded by actual G.S.P. trade. Consequently, it is unlikely that actual G.S.P. imports of semi-sensitive products will exceed a limit without the cessation of G.S.P. tariff treatment. On the other hand, it is quite possible for G.S.P. tariffs to apply on other non-sensitive items even beyond the ceiling or maximum-amount limits.

The administration of G.S.P. trade in sensitive products is much more rigid. All of these products have been predefined with ceiling, maximum-amount, and member-state allocation limits precalculated and circulated to member states. Actual G.S.P. imports are very closely monitored for the immediate and automatic re-establishment of M.F.N. duties when any limit is met. Contrary to the case with non-sensitive products, there is no time lag in administrative procedure, starting with the domestic producer and proceeding through member-state governments to the E.E.C. Commission. Instead, with sensitive products the ultimate administration takes place at the member-state level with each member state being responsible for the administration of its share of the Community ceiling. And this member-state responsibility includes the right to predesignate those importers who are entitled to import under G.S.P. privileges.

In order to fully appreciate the constraints embodied in this ceiling system we must examine the techniques used to administer G.S.P. trade in the various member states. For example, West Germany uses two types of administrative procedure.

(1) *First-come, first-served:* shipments are cleared through customs under G.S.P. tariffs and charged to the German allocation in the order in which they are physically presented until the allocation is fully utilised. Such an arrangement benefits those importers who are best able to 'race' goods to the border once the ceiling is opened at the beginning of each year. This tends to favour the large and experienced importers who either hold inventory stocks in nearby off-shore warehouses or who import from rather advanced and closely located beneficiary countries.

(2) *Prior allocation:* specific importers, generally based on past trading behaviour, are issued G.S.P. import permits up to the German allocation. Once a permit has been received, the importer is guaranteed the right to import under G.S.P. tariffs without having to race the goods in. Each permit specifies the product, permissible G.S.P. volume, and generally additional conditions such as time limits, and so on. Unused permits are to be returned to the issuing agency for reallocation to an alternative importer. In cases where the German allocation is less than the expected volume of imports from beneficiaries, the allocated importers are given a pseudo monopsony position; thus we can anticipate that the G.S.P. tariff saving on such products will end up in the importers' pockets rather than serve as an inducement for expanded trade flows (which are prohibited by the allocation limit). Although the member-state allocation, and hence the Community ceiling, is locally administered, the maximum amount is administered at the Community level on a first-come, first-served basis.

Benelux operates its G.S.P. on a first-come, first-served basis. The major problem here is the uncertainty aspect and consequential risk of M.F.N. duties being charged. This risk is especially significant to the large 'trading houses' – which efficiently operate on rather small profit margins in order to maintain their price competitiveness.

The French operate almost entirely on the prior allocation basis. But unlike West Germany, France allocates permits in consultation with ministries and representatives of domestic producers. Often the importers will have close ties with domestic producers, in some cases even being the domestic producers. This may explain why the French allocation often remains largely unused.

Another aspect of the uncertainty element has important implications for the longer-run objectives of the G.S.P. We have already seen that the tariff treatment which will actually apply when the goods are cleared through customs introduces a risk element to importers that can be expected to affect their willingness to contract for beneficiary exports. Thus each year importers must re-evaluate the attractiveness of beneficiary products in light of the recalculated ceilings and current trade volumes.

It was also hoped that the G.S.P. would provide a stimulus to investment in new productive capacity in developing countries. Obviously the uncertainty element dampens this stimulus as well. There is, moreover, an additional uncertainty element that investors must consider. Each year when the ceilings are re-opened, the E.E.C. changes the classification of some product groups. This might result in some sensitive products with grossly 'open-ended' ceilings being reclassified as semi-sensitive or strictly non-sensitive. Unfortunately, however, the main scrutiny for possible reclassification concerns troublesome products, i.e. non-sensitive or semi-sensitive items having unexpectedly large trade flows which could be prevented by tighter controls. Thus the greatest likelihood for reclassification is for non-sensitive items to be reclassified as semi-sensitive or sensitive and for semi-sensitive products to be reclassified as sensitive.

In conclusion, the tendency within the ceiling system is for: (1) the ceiling, maximum-amount and member-state allocation limits to become more restrictive (as trade grows faster than ceilings grow); and (2) the administration to become more immediate, automatic and rigid as product groups are reclassified from non-sensitive to semi-sensitive to sensitive.

JAPAN'S ADMINISTRATION OF G.S.P. TRADE

As is the case with the E.E.C., Japan's system of ceilings governs G.S.P. trade in industrial products only; producers of agricultural and fishery products are protected via a more traditional escape clause. For administration purposes, the industrial items are classified into roughly 200 product groups, with G.S.P. trade in each group controlled according to one of three methods – daily control, monthly control or prior allocation.

Under the daily-control method, preferential treatment is granted to imports of G.S.P. products on a first-come, first-served basis. The value of preferential imports is reported and accumulated daily; preferential treatment will be suspended two days after a ceiling or maximum-amount limit is met. Roughly 40 per cent of the product groups (accounting for 50 per cent of G.S.P. trade) fall under daily control. The monthly-control method differs from the daily-control method only in the timing of monitoring and G.S.P. tariff suspension. Preferential trade is reported monthly and preferential tariff treatment is suspended on the first day of the second month after a ceiling or maximum-amount limit is met. For example, a ceiling which is exceeded during the month of July will be reported as such in August; and the M.F.N. tariff rate will be reinstated on 1 September. Approximately half of the product groups come under this method of control accounting for 40 per cent of beneficiary trade. G.S.P. trade in the remaining eleven product groups is administered via G.S.P. import permits which the government has, in advance, allotted to importers. Recently Japan introduced a more flexible administration of the ceiling and maximum-amount limits which provides that G.S.P. tariff treatment need not be automatically withdrawn when one of the limits is reached. The flexible administration applies to roughly half of the product groups, i.e. those products considered to provide little threat to domestic producers even if permitted access under G.S.P. treatment.

Obviously the Japanese system of ceilings contains uncertainty elements similar to those of the E.E.C. The government does reduce this uncertainty element somewhat by publishing the total level of preferential trade in each product group on a monthly basis. Since the ceilings are also made public, importers can get some indication of the likelihood that a particular product group will face a G.S.P. tariff suspension. However, such information does not help much in identifying when a particular maximum-amount limit will become operative. Moreover, even the total preferential trade reporting may be misleading if trade is seasonal or if imports tend to be received in large sporadic shipments.

SAFEGUARD MEASURES OF THE UNITED STATES

The legislation authorising the U.S. preferential tariff system is extremely complex – more so than that authorising any of the other industrial nation's G.S.P. schemes. This complexity is due in part to the separation of powers between the legislative and executive branches of government as spelled out in the U.S. Constitution. In essence, Congress empowers the President to administer programmes deemed desirable to Congress. In the case of foreign policy, the President is responsible for initiating action but must obtain congressional consent on any matter dealing with the expenditure or receipt of monies. Since the G.S.P. results in a reduction of certain import taxes (tariff rates), the President must obtain prior approval from Congress – such approval is contained in the Trade Act of 1974.

A second factor contributing to the complexity of the law was simply the time that it was brought before Congress – a time when U.S.–Soviet Union relations were coming under strain because of the Jewish immigration problem, a time when Congress was wrestling with a new energy problem to combat the new-found power of the Arab nations, and a time when the North–South confrontation was giving rise to an increase in tension.

The combining of these political factors with the general world-wide recession (high unemployment in the United States) and intense congressional concern to prevent presidential usurpation of power (as evidenced by the Watergate affair) led to a very carefully written Trade Act. Even so, Congress realised that it should not legislate a rigid G.S.P. because of rapidly changing world events. Instead flexibility was provided to cope with new unforeseen conditions. The compromise between limiting the President's discretionary power and providing the desired flexibility was inserted into the Act in the form of conditions which the President must consider in administering the U.S. G.S.P. as well as a presidential obligation to inform Congress of the discretionary decisions taken.

The limitations on presidential power were quite rigid regarding the selection of developing countries and products to come under the G.S.P. provisions (as was discussed in the previous two chapters). When it came to safeguarding domestic firms and workers, the limits are generally one way only. The President has rather wide discretionary powers to limit or restrict G.S.P. tariff treatment but much less latitude to allow G.S.P. tariffs when there is any hint of threat to domestic producers.

The Trade Act makes no specific mention of a separate safeguard clause applicable to G.S.P. trade. Nevertheless, there are several implicit and explicit provisions to protect domestic producers. In the first place, the President has the discretionary authority to delete any article from the preference provisions with respect to one or more beneficiary countries.* This authority gives him an extremely wide range of options for protecting domestic interests. In addition, there are a number of situations in which the President *is required* to restrict the G.S.P. In these cases the relationship between G.S.P. trade flows and economic injury to a domestic producer or group of workers is irrelevant.† Similarly the interests of U.S. importers or consumers are irrelevant. The two major cases in which the President is obliged to restrict G.S.P. trade concern (1) the 'competitive-need' criteria, and (2) import-relief action under section 203 of the Trade Act of 1974.

U.S. competitive-need criteria

The competitive-need criteria provide for the automatic withdrawal of preferential treatment whenever U.S. imports of a particular product from a particular beneficiary country exceed either (1) $25 million annually, or (2) 50 per cent of total U.S. imports of the product.‡ In administering these

---

* The President also has the power to increase the list of beneficiaries or products, but this power is limited in both instances and, moreover, requires the President to give ample opportunity for opposing views to be aired in public. Finally, he must also notify Congress of such modifications in the G.S.P. (see Chapters 3 and 4).

† An understandable though insignificant example is that any product that becomes subject to a 'National Security' trade restriction (under section 232 of the Trade Expansion Act of 1962) must be removed from the G.S.P. Presently this provision affects trade in only a few petroleum products.

‡ Each year the $25 million limit will be increased in proportion to the previous year's growth in the U.S. gross national product. This growth factor provides an inflation hedge plus an increase related to the 'real growth' in U.S. production.

criteria no distinction is made between imports which actually received G.S.P. tariff treatment and imports which did not, for example due to the failure to apply for G.S.P. treatment or due to the rules of origin (see Chapter 6). Nor is this provision similar to the ceiling limits of the E.E.C. or Japan whereby the ceilings are re-opened at the beginning of each new year; instead, once a competitive need limit is exceeded, the involved beneficiary exporters cease to enjoy G.S.P. tariffs on the product beginning sixty days after the close of the following calendar year. The affected beneficiary country does continue to enjoy G.S.P. preferential treatment on other products and other beneficiary countries will continue to enjoy G.S.P. tariff treatment on the particular product. There are, however, three exceptions to a permanent loss of preferential tariff treatment:

(1) if during a subsequent year the 'competitive-need' limit is not met, G.S.P. tariff treatment will be reinstated;

(2) there is a special competitive-need criteria waiver for the Philippines because of its historical preferential ties with the United States;* and

(3) the 50 per cent limit is non-operative for articles which were not produced in the United States at the time the U.S. G.S.P. was first passed into law (3 January 1975).†

The primary rationale underlying these so-called 'competitive-need' criteria is that developing countries do not need preferential tariff treatment on products which are exported competitively under M.F.N. treatment. Given that the various developing countries are often competitive in different products, a degree of flexibility is required so that only those developing countries which are competitive in a particular product fail to receive G.S.P. tariff treatment.

A second rationale is to provide for the removal of preferences in those cases where G.S.P. tariff treatment is no longer necessary, i.e. when the developing country can compete in world markets. The ultimate objective, therefore, is to phase out the G.S.P. as developing countries industrialise.

And finally, an interrelated rationale is that domestic producers can withstand increased competition from newly established developing-country producers. But as these producers develop beyond the stage of an infant industry, gaining sophistication in industrial production and marketing, domestic producers will begin to be adversely affected – especially in those

---

* In the Executive Order implementing the U.S. G.S.P. on 1 January 1976, the Philippines was designated as a beneficiary which would *not* receive G.S.P. tariff treatment on ten different product groups.

† Since G.S.P. products are defined at the five-digit U.S. Tariff Schedule (T.S.U.S.) level of aggregation, few beneficiaries are likely to gain from this exception; the broad industrial base of the United States results in domestic production in nearly every five-digit T.S.U.S. product category.

cases where labour costs are important. Moreover, even if domestic producers could compete (since domestic producers do not pay duties either),
the preferential tariff treatment would lead to a significant distortion of U.S.
imports away from traditional sources of supply – the industrial nations of
the West. Although the G.S.P. was designed to assist developing countries, it
was not offered with the intent of adversely affecting trade among the
Western countries.

This does, however, raise the question of how to define international
competitiveness. Is it true that a developing-country industry is competitive
in world markets when it supplies $25 million annually to the United States
or when it supplies over half of the U.S. import demand? For some industries both of these criteria may be justifiable. But for all? Remember that for
the purpose of the G.S.P., industries are defined in accordance with the U.S.
Tariff Schedule (T.S.U.S.). The T.S.U.S. has some 10,000 five-digit tariff lines
for defining products at varying levels of aggregation. For broadly defined
product groups a particular developing country may exceed the $25 million
limit as a result of many firms exporting somewhat different products to the
United States – all falling within the same five-digit T.S.U.S. product
category; and for narrowly defined product groups the 50 per cent limit
might be exceeded even though a rather small volume of trade is involved.
The problem is that the tariff schedules were defined for purposes of administering import duties, not for the purpose of defining competitiveness in
world markets. If the application of the T.S.U.S. definitions are necessary
for administrative purposes, their shortcomings for defining competitiveness
should be recognised and incorporated into the competitive-need criteria.
Rather than adopt an automatic mechanism with such variable effects, it
would seem more reasonable to use these two limits as warning signals
instead. The withdrawal of G.S.P. tariff treatment could be decided on a
case-by-case basis after examining the degree of injury to domestic producers and the ability of the developing-country supplier to compete in
world (rather than U.S.) markets.

But in any event, the competitive-need criteria as specified in the law do
not provide for the commercial interests of domestic producers; the clause
which does involves import-relief measures.

Import-relief action

The Trade Act specified that G.S.P. tariff treatment must be suspended on
any product which becomes subject to any import-relief action *proclaimed*
under section 203.* This provides for the prevention or correction of serious
injury or threat thereof to a domestic industry; the President is empowered:

---

* A similar provision applies to those products currently subject to escape-clause action under
section 351 of the Trade Expansion Act of 1962. However, no new escape-clause action is
possible as this clause has been superseded by the import-relief measures of the 1974 Act.

(1) to *proclaim* an increase in tariff on the product;

(2) to *proclaim* a tariff quota;

(3) to *proclaim* a quantitative restriction on imports; or

(4) to *negotiate* an orderly marketing agreement.

The word *proclaim* is crucial. If import-relief action is warranted and the President chooses to protect domestic producers by negotiating an orderly marketing agreement, G.S.P. tariff treatment need not cease. A similar interpretation applies to other country-specific measures such as anti-dumping action, countervailing duty impositions, voluntary export restrictions, and so on. Only when the import-relief measure is applied on a most-favoured-nation basis is it necessary to suspend G.S.P. tariff treatment on the product involved.* But in this case all beneficiary developing countries will cease to enjoy preferential tariff treatment; and this action is independent of the source of the troublesome imports. It is this last point that makes the import-relief clause so unfortunate. Rather than this automatic tie between import-relief action and the cessation of G.S.P. tariff treatment, it would be much preferable to have a causal tie relating G.S.P. imports and injury to a domestic producer or group of workers. As it now stands, G.S.P. tariff treatment could be suspended even in cases where developing-country trade in a troublesome product accounts for a minuscule share of the domestic market.

This criticism of the U.S. import-relief measure can also be applied to the 'competitive-need' criteria and to the ceiling systems of the E.E.C. and Japan. Under all three schemes, G.S.P. tariff treatment automatically ceases when G.S.P. trade exceeds a predetermined limit; and the particular limits are unrelated to the viability of domestic import-competing industries. It is not surprising that such an automatic safeguard which operates without any direct tie to injury to domestic producers or workers is much more restrictive than necessary. In order to safeguard injured sectors without unduly limiting G.S.P. trade, a more flexible measure is needed – one that is based on a causal tie between injury and increased G.S.P. trade. Such a causal tie is an integral part of the traditional escape clause embodied in the articles of GATT.

Finally, in addition to the specific ceiling-type safeguards, the reservation clause whereby donors can withdraw or modify their respective G.S.P. schemes as they choose, and the exclusion of 'sensitive' products, G.S.P. trade is subject to numerous non-tariff barriers to trade – many of which apply to M.F.N. trade as well. Mention has already been made of the case of the E.E.C. granting G.S.P. preferences on imports of textiles provided the

---

* It should also be pointed out that many of the products currently subject to escape-clause action under the 1962 Act come under the adjustment assistance provisions rather than most-favoured-nation tariff or quota treatment. In such cases G.S.P. tariff treatment is not precluded by the 1974 Act.

exporting beneficiary country abides by the provisions of the Long Term Arrangement for Trade in Textiles (the recently renewed L.T.A.). The E.E.C. also grants G.S.P. treatment on a number of agricultural products. However, the G.S.P. tariff reduction does not apply to the 'variable-levy' component of the duty which is adjusted daily to maintain a price advantage (over the international price) in favour of domestic producers.

With the conclusion of the Kennedy Round of tariff negotiations, M.F.N. duties have been so reduced that tariffs are no longer a serious barrier to trade. This is evidenced by a rapidly changing commodity pattern of international trade among the developed countries. We have also witnessed a significant expansion in the exportation of non-traditional products by developing countries. These events normally lead to increased pressure for domestic adjustments to increased import competition. Such adjustments are always troublesome for some sectors and some relatively immobile resources – but less so when both domestic and international markets are expanding rapidly, as during the 1960s. But with the world-wide recession of the mid-1970s, the pressures for adjustment to increased import competition became unbearable. Since the GATT procedures make it difficult to introduce increased tariff protection, the industrial nations have turned to more subtle non-tariff techniques to safeguard the interests of their domestic producers and workers. It is difficult to predict where this new trend will take us, but there is little doubt that the export prospects of the developing countries, even with their new-found advantages under the G.S.P., will be injured.

6

Rules of Origin

The primary objective of the G.S.P. is to stimulate production and employment in export sectors of the developing countries. However, preferential tariff rates as a stimulus might lead to a different result, namely a deflection of international trade among industrial countries. Instead of one industrial nation exporting goods directly to another and facing M.F.N. tariffs, the exporter might send the goods first to a beneficiary developing country for importation and immediate re-exportation to the initially intended industrial nation, thereby gaining customs clearance under G.S.P. tariff rates. In this way the G.S.P. could initiate a system of trade diversion through beneficiary countries, stimulating the creation of 'trading houses' rather than industrial production and employment. It is true that a certain degree of 'paper-processing' employment and income would be generated in the developing countries, but the benefits of such economic activity would fall far short of the G.S.P. objectives of industrialisation and acceleration of economic growth. To prevent such a deflection of trade, 'rules of origin' were established. These rules constitute a set of requirements designed to prevent the beneficiaries from simply re-exporting goods produced elsewhere unless such goods were substantially processed in the exporting beneficiary developing country.

In general, these rules specify three conditions that must be met before exporting goods will qualify for G.S.P. tariff treatment:

(1) the goods must be shipped directly from the beneficiary developing country to the donor country without intermediate processing or trading (direct consignment);

(2) the goods must be accompanied by appropriate documentation which certifies that they qualify for G.S.P. tariff treatment; and

(3) the goods must undergo minimum processing in the beneficiary developing country.

These conditions will be treated in turn.

DIRECT CONSIGNMENT

For goods to be regarded as directly consigned to the donor country they must be shipped directly from the beneficiary developing country without passing through the territory of any other country. But such a requirement would be impossible for certain beneficiary countries to meet; specifically, land-locked countries must tranship their exports through third countries.* To accommodate such countries, the consignment rules permit tranship-ment provided the goods remain under customs transit control and do not enter into trade or consumption in third countries. While in transit the goods may not undergo further processing, packaging, and so on, other than unloading, reloading, splitting up of loads, or special operations required to keep them in good condition. Often such transhipment is permitted only when justified by geographical reasons or conditions relating exclusively to transportation requirements. And finally, this rule is often accompanied by a requirement that at the time the goods leave the exporting beneficiary developing country the exporter must identify the donor country to which the goods are going.

Such a direct-consignment rule poses little problem for most of the beneficiary developing countries, especially the major exporters. However, experience has indicated that for land-locked countries, even this require-ment is insufficient to meet their needs. Often the major marketing opera-tions for a land-locked country take place in a neighbouring country's seaport city. The export item is transhipped to the seaport city for warehous-ing until an appropriate buyer has been identified. Further, if the buyer requires specific packaging or labelling (which might depend on the langu-age of the destination country), such preparations for exportation would take place in the neighbouring country rather than in the exporting beneficiary country. Some of the donor countries do not permit even such warehousing in a neighbouring country prior to sale; others permit this but do not permit special packaging to suit the needs of the ultimate buyer. At the very least, this direct-consignment rule should be liberalised to accom-modate these types of marketing needs of the land-locked beneficiaries.

Moreover, if the beneficiary exporters are to take advantage of the most attractive market when the goods arrive at their destination (as opposed to when they were originally shipped), it is necessary to allow for more flexibi-lity in shipment, for example to permit changing the final destination, tran-shipment through non-predesignated third countries, sub-dividing a shipment with parts going to various final markets, and so on. Such flexibi-lity is necessary if the beneficiary exports are to compete with the sophist-icated market and distribution techniques of producers in the developed countries. So long as the goods are not further processed after leaving the beneficiary country (other than, say, minor packaging to meet the needs of the final consumers), such flexibility in shipment seems reasonable and con-sistent with the purposes of the direct-consignment rule. After all, the only

---

* For example, Afghanistan, Bhutan, Bolivia, Burindi, Central African Republic, Chad, Laos, Lesotho, Mali, Nepal, Niger, Paraguay, Rwanda, Sikkim, Swaziland, Uganda, Upper Volta and Zambia.

purpose of the direct-consignment rule is to ensure that the identity of goods claimed to be eligible for G.S.P. tariff treatment can be traced back to their original export source.

DOCUMENTARY EVIDENCE

The documentary-evidence rule is designed to ensure that goods presented for customs clearance under G.S.P. tariff treatment are, in fact, entitled to such preferential treatment. The documentation (certificate of origin, or 'Form A') contains information to substantiate the claim that the goods have originated in a particular beneficiary developing country and have met the substantial transformation requirements. The certificates of origin are prepared by the beneficiary exporter and certified by an agency predesignated by the beneficiary government.

Each of the donor countries have required that each beneficiary government communicate to them the name of each agency authorised to issue certificates of origin and impressions of the official stamps which will be used to validate the certificates. The failure to notify the donor countries of the authorising agencies and official stamps would mean a loss of G.S.P. tariff treatment.

During the early stages of the G.S.P., many beneficiaries had difficulties in meeting this requirement. However, the combined efforts of the donor-country governments, the beneficiary-country governments and the UNCTAD Secretariat have largely solved this problem. Some donor countries even establish interim procedures to grant provisional G.S.P. tariff treatment for goods presented for customs clearance without all appropriate documentation.* By now, those remaining beneficiaries which have not fully complied with the notification requirement tend to be minor suppliers of products covered by the respective preference schemes.

MINIMAL PROCESSING

Minimal-processing requirements have been established by each donor country to ensure that goods clearing customs under G.S.P. tariff treatment are actually produced in the exporting beneficiary country rather than simply imported from a developed country and re-exported. But these rules do recognise that developing-country production processes may often be dependent on imported materials or components. In general, the minimal-processing requirement is expressed as an 'either or' test; either the goods

---

* If appropriate documentation is not presented within a prespecified time period, the importer was required to pay the M.F.N. duty. Normally provisional treatment was granted after the importer posted a bond guaranteeing M.F.N. duty; sometimes the full M.F.N. duty was initially paid but was subject to rebate when the documentation arrived.

presented for G.S.P. tariff treatment are (1) wholly produced in the exporting beneficiary developing country,* or (2) substantially transformed from imported materials and components.

In theory the definition of wholly produced goods is clear cut. A wholly produced good is derived from a production process using no imported materials or components; thus all inputs must themselves be produced in the beneficiary developing country. Any tools or machinery used in the production process but not embodied in the final goods are ignored. However, in practice a few definitional problems do exist. In the case of marine products made on board factory ships, donors have disagreed on what constitutes 'wholly produced'. Some donors grant G.S.P. tariff treatment on goods imported from any factory ship registered in a beneficiary developing country; other donors require in addition that the factory ship fly the flag of the same beneficiary country; and still other donors require that the captain, officers and at least 75 per cent of the crew be nationals of the beneficiary country. The exports of factory ships chartered by developing countries are generally not treated as wholly produced for purposes of the G.S.P. In other cases, products obtained from live animals are sometimes excluded from G.S.P. tariff treatment if the live animals were at one time imported into the beneficiary country – instead it is required that the live animals be born and raised in the exporting beneficiary country.

The major controversy surrounding the rules of origin involves the question of what constitutes *substantial transformation*: just how much must imported materials be transformed before the final goods can be considered to be produced in the exporting beneficiary country?† Of course, the objective of such a requirement is to ensure that the G.S.P. contributes to the process of industrialisation and economic growth in the developing countries. The donor countries have defined the concept of substantial transformation in two ways. Austria, the E.E.C., Finland, Japan, Norway, Sweden and Switzerland base their definition on what is called the 'process' criterion, whereas Australia, Canada, New Zealand and the United States have adopted a 'value-added' criterion.

The principle underlying the process criterion is that the final goods must be defined for tariff purposes as different than any imported materials or components embodied in them. Since the countries which use this concept base their tariff schedules on the Brussels Tariff Nomenclature (B.T.N.), a change of product definition is met when the final good falls under a different four-digit B.T.N. product category (tariff heading) than any imported materials or components used in the production process. However, certain

* The U.S. scheme, as authorised under the Trade Act of 1974, makes no special provision for wholly produced goods. This point is discussed later in this section.
† To put things in their proper perspective, over three-quarters of G.S.P. trade involves wholly produced goods. However, for many specific products the question of permissible import content is crucial.

exceptions occur in which a product undergoes a change of tariff heading after only superficial transformation, for example simple mixing of two or more items, or the simple assembly of parts to make a complete article; in such cases, G.S.P. tariff treatment does not apply. On the other hand, there are a number of cases in which substantial transformation has occurred without a change in tariff heading; such cases do meet the origin requirements. As happened so often in negotiating the G.S.P., countries could not agree on every exception, so each donor using the process criterion has its own set of exceptions to the general 'change of tariff heading' rule: one set of processes which do not qualify goods for G.S.P. treatment even though a change of tariff heading did occur (so-called List A);* and another set of processes which do qualify even though no change of B.T.N. category occurred (List B). These lists of exceptions are quite extensive and sophisticated; for example, Lists A and B of the E.E.C. involve some eighty-five pages of technical specifications. The developing countries will have tremendous difficulty in understanding (let alone administering) these rules.

The normal complexities of these lists of exceptions are greatly compounded by each donor specifying a separate set of exceptions; moreover, the donors often incorporated requirements designed to protect domestic producers. As a result various products have been *de facto* excluded from G.S.P. tariff treatment by respective donors specifying minimum-processing requirements which the developing countries cannot meet. For example, transistor radios do not qualify for G.S.P. tariff treatment in the E.E.C. if they are made using imported transistors, which few if any developing countries can domestically produce. Thus for all practical purposes the E.E.C. does not grant preferences on transistor radios. Also, until recently modified, plastic goods qualified only if they were manufactured from imported basic chemicals but not if from imported plastic materials. To a certain degree the developing countries were required to have a domestic petro-chemicals industry.

The major problem caused by the process criterion is that there is really no general rule to be followed. The lists of exceptions are so broad that for all practical purposes each product must be treated individually. Each exporter must examine not only the 'change of tariff heading' but also the particular 'process' which is used to produce the final good. Moreover, since the rules differ from donor to donor, he must note the particular regulations for the destination donor country as well. It would be far preferable if all donors using the process definition adopted the same lists of exceptions; but since different countries have different international trade problems, and therefore tariff structures, the best that we can hope for is that these donors harmonise their lists to the greatest extent possible.

* List A sometimes specified additional processing requirements which must be met instead of outright exclusion from G.S.P. tariff treatment. For example, the good might qualify only if the value of imported materials is less than 50 per cent of the value of the final good.

The only case in which the process criterion poses little problem is when the good is wholly produced and therefore does not embody any imported materials or components. Fortunately for the developing countries, most of the products exported are wholly produced.

In contrast to the process criterion, the value-added criterion used by Australia, Canada, New Zealand and the United States is much more general, although it does differ from donor to donor. In essence, the value-added criterion simply places a maximum limit on the use of imported inputs in the production process, so that the value of imported materials and components cannot exceed a certain percentage (say 50 per cent) of the export value of the final good. Canada has specified just such a value-added rule. New Zealand adopted the same criterion, though stated it in the converse: 'total domestic costs, including the value of materials and components originating in the same beneficiary country but excluding imported materials and components, must not be less than half the total cost of the export good'.* Even though these formulations make no special provision for wholly produced goods, such goods obviously qualify for G.S.P. tariff treatment; in the case of wholly produced goods, the percentage of imported materials and components is zero.

The value-added criterion of the United States introduces a new twist. Instead of specifying a maximum limit on the use of imported materials and components, as did Canada, the United States followed the minimum local value-added precedent of New Zealand. But more importantly, the value-added criterion is defined in terms of direct costs of processing. More specifically, G.S.P. tariff treatment will apply only

if the sum of (i) the cost or value of the materials produced in the beneficiary developing country plus (ii) the direct costs of processing operations performed in such beneficiary developing country is not less than 35% of the export value.[1]

This direct processing concept evolved out of a trade arrangement with the Virgin Islands regarding watches which are assembled in the Virgin Islands for sale in the United States. The arrangement originally provided that a limited number of watches (set by quota) could be assembled in the Virgin Islands using non-U.S. watch parts and sold in the United States provided the value of the imported components did not exceed 50 per cent of the final export value of the watch.

Over time, the cost of the imported components rose to the point where this 50 per cent requirement could not be met. Since the assembly plant was owned by a U.S. firm, the export price of the watches could be increased

* New Zealand also includes any materials and components imported from New Zealand as counting towards the beneficiary-country value-added requirement.

without affecting the over-all profit position of the firm (the Virgin Island plant profits were increased by an amount equal to the profit decline of the U.S. parent firm). As the export price of the watches increased, the more expensive components would still fall within the 50 per cent requirement. Thus, by altering the intra-firm transfer price of watches, thereby increasing profits, the 50 per cent requirement could always be met. This loop-hole in the trade arrangement was closed by establishing customs regulations which excluded profits from the export value of the watches.

Rather than settling the issue, the closing of this loop-hole stimulated the corporation's search for another. The firm simply set up executive offices with name plates for corporate officers who worked for the U.S. parent corporation but who never set foot in the Virgin Islands and whose salaries were paid out of the Virgin Island plant's account. In this way the expenses of the Virgin Island plant were increased (without any cost to the firm since these salaries were now being saved by the parent office). As the plant's expenses were higher, the export price of watches could be increased without increasing profits, and again the 50 per cent requirement could be met. Thus executive salaries must also be excluded from the export value of watches in order to effectively close the loop-hole through which a multinational firm could perpetually circumvent the 50 per cent requirement. But obviously there are a host of other techniques available to such firms to increase the costs of the Virgin Island plant without affecting the profit position of the firm. To name a few: an intra-company loan from the parent to the Virgin Island plant at a very high interest rate (thus interest payments must also be excluded from the export value); the establishment of a licensing fee or royalty payment from off-shore plant to parent for 'technology' used in assembling watches (thus excluding licensing fees and royalties); attribute the distribution and selling costs in the United States to the Virgin Island plant (thus excluding export selling expenses); and so on. The range of such possibilities is almost without limit.

In order to effectively close this loop-hole, the customs definition of the export value must exclude any off-shore plant cost that can be shifted from parent to off-shore plant without affecting the corporation's over-all profit position: and thus the concept of 'direct costs of processing operations plus domestically produced materials and components'. In fact, the U.S. adoption of this origin concept emphasises a fear that U.S. multinational corporations may respond strongly to the G.S.P. price incentives and transfer productive capacity from the United States to beneficiary developing countries, thereby exporting jobs.

But what about the significance of this direct processing cost concept to the beneficiary exporters? In the first place, unlike the value-added concepts adopted by Canada and New Zealand, wholly produced articles might not meet the 35 per cent requirement, i.e. when indirect costs exceed 65 per cent of the export value. For example, based on 1967 data published by the

United Nations,[2] Portland Cement produced in East Africa would not meet this requirement even if wholly produced – due to large royalty payments and profits.

In the second place, even if this *de facto* exclusion of wholly produced items proves to be valid in theory but not in practice, the direct processing costs concept does significantly reduce the scope for using imported materials and components. For example, consider a product having an export value of $100, of which $50 is direct processing costs, including locally produced materials and components, and $50 is indirect costs. The 35 per cent requirement means that at most only $15 worth of imported components can be used (the $50 direct costs less $35 origin required). Hence only 15 per cent of the export value can be accounted for by imported materials and components. This and other variations of this theme are presented in Table 6.1. The examples shown in the table illustrate the strong inverse relationship between indirect costs and the maximum permissible import content. A one percentage point increase in the share of indirect costs reduces the maximum import content by one percentage point.

TABLE 6.1

Export value	$100	$100	$100	$100
Indirect cost	66	50	40	25
Minimum domestic processing costs	35	35	35	35
Maximum import content	*	15	25	40
Effective value-added requirement†	—	85	75	60

* Such a product cannot meet the 35 per cent requirement even if wholly produced.
† An x per cent maximum import content can be roughly translated into an $(100-x)$ 'effective value-added' concept since the bulk of indirect costs will be domestically generated.

But to be fair to the United States, the degree of stringency of this new form of the origin requirement cannot be derived from what is explicitly contained in the authorising legislation. Moreover, there is sufficient range for administrative discretion that projections based on what is implicitly contained in the Trade Act are also likely to be somewhat off base. Nevertheless, there is a history of U.S. custom law and court interpretations that shed some light on the likely administration of some elements of this origin requirement. For example, direct processing costs will probably include such items as operating labour costs, including fringe benefits, supervisory and quality-control personnel, depreciation on machinery, and research and development expenses; it will probably exclude profits, administrative salaries, overhead expenses, utilities, maintenance and repairs, selling expenses, licensing fees and royalties. This leaves a host of other expense items whose assignment to direct versus indirect costs must be decided by customs officials; at this date it is impossible to know precisely how such an assignment will be made or, in fact, how restrictive this new variation of the value-added origin concept will be. Only time can tell.

At this early stage in the development of a new world preferential trade policy in favour of developing countries, one should not be too critical of the particular rules of origin adopted by the donor countries; nor should one expect the administrative procedures to be excessively stringent. Instead customs officials can be expected to be relatively lenient in their administration of G.S.P. trade, although, on the other hand, we must also expect them to operate within the respective laws and regulations governing such trade. In this regard, the U.S. direct processing costs requirement is unfortunate. At the very least there should be a very simple procedure for granting G.S.P. tariff treatment to wholly produced articles; and, second, since the purpose of the rules of origin is to limit the use of imported materials, the origin requirement should be based on an import-content criterion such as 'the value of imported materials and components cannot exceed a certain percentage of the export value of the final product'. Alternatively, if the United States is concerned about the opportunity of multinational corporations to influence indirect costs, the import-content criterion might be specified thus: 'the value of imported materials and components cannot exceed a certain percentage of direct processing costs plus the value of locally produced material inputs'. But in the latter case the base value for calculating the maximum import content is smaller; consequently, the maximum percentage requirement should be larger.

In the final analysis the rules of origin pose a 'be damned if you do and be damned if you don't' dilemma. The objective of the G.S.P. is to provide a new and additional incentive to stimulate industrialisation in developing countries. Origin rules which are extremely liberal and thereby easy for developing countries to meet would be full of loop-holes, thus facilitating the diversion of developed-country trade through beneficiary countries. The outcome would be the creation of low value-added 'trading houses' with relatively minor employment opportunities and little if any real incentive for industrial activity. On the other hand, extremely rigid rules which would maximise the incentive for industrial employment are likely to be self-defeating by specifying conditions which few if any developing countries can satisfy. It is not too surprising that the initial rules adopted differ from donor to donor and fall within a nebulous middle ground. Nor should it be surprising that a number of particular rules are found to be too rigid; obviously some others are too lenient but who is going to complain – certainly not the profit-making 'trading house' operator. A responsible evaluation of the rules of origin presently in force, given the existing imperfections in knowledge and political influence, may conclude that for a start they are not too bad. A negotiation forum does exist in the UNCTAD Special Committee on Preferences. Controversial issues are being discussed and, in fact, some improvements in the rules of origin have taken place. Over time we can reasonably hope that acceptably workable rules will evolve.

CUMULATIVE ORIGIN

There does remain one major area of inconsistency between the objectives of the G.S.P. and the requirements of the rules of origin. Generally, the rules of origin limit the import content of G.S.P. exports regardless of the source of the imported materials and components.* But those cases in which the imported materials and components originated in another beneficiary country provide the same stimulus for industrialisation in developing countries. In fact, it seems most logical to treat all beneficiary developing countries as a single unit for purposes of determining origin. Thus the processing which occurs in one beneficiary would be added to that occurring in others to arrive at a total developing-country content, i.e. cumulative origin.

Such cumulative treatment would recognise the realities of industrial production and the existing levels of industrialisation in many developing countries. Industrial activity in the less advanced developing countries is heavily dependent on imported materials and components if they are to produce anything other than simple semi-manufactured articles. But under cumulative treatment such countries could enter into basic assembly-type operations provided the components originated in another developing country. In this way, cumulative origin could facilitate international specialisation, based on comparative advantage, among the developing countries.

When the G.S.P. was first introduced in late 1971 and early 1972, there were no provisions for cumulative origin. But in subsequent UNCTAD deliberations the issue was raised. As a result, the E.E.C. recently modified its origin rules to provide for cumulative treatment within three recognised regional groupings of developing countries (the Association of South East Asian Nations, the Central American Common Market and the Andean Group). Under the U.S. scheme, cumulative origin is permissible for those developing-country associations which are formal free-trade areas or customs unions. Such components and materials produced in one member developing country and used by another will be counted towards meeting the minimum-processing requirement under the origin rules.

There are, however, certain strings attached to the U.S. cumulative origin provision. First, for such an association the minimum-processing requirement is increased from 35 per cent of the export value of the article to 50 per cent; such an increase is not insignificant since the United States bases its minimum-processing requirement on direct processing costs rather than the

---

* Japan treats all materials and components imported from Japan as originating in the particular exporting beneficiary country; New Zealand has a similar provision.

total export value of the product. The second disadvantage of the cumulative origin treatment is that the 'competitive-need' limitations apply to the association as a group rather than to the individual member countries. If annual U.S. imports of a given product from all beneficiary members of an association combined exceed $25 million or 50 per cent of total U.S. imports of the product, G.S.P. tariff treatment will be terminated for all beneficiaries belonging to the association; and such preferential treatment is terminated even for a beneficiary which accounts for only a minor trade flow, measured either in value or percentage terms. Cumulative treatment under such conditions is hardly better than no cumulative treatment at all.

7

Evaluation of the G.S.P. in Operation

In the previous four chapters I have described and tentatively evaluated the numerous institutional aspects of the entire G.S.P. system. This discussion concentrated on the so-called 'big three' schemes – those of the E.E.C., Japan and the United States – which together will account for some 90 per cent of all G.S.P. trade. In this chapter, the prior analysis will be carried one step further. I will attempt to evaluate the G.S.P. based upon *ex ante* quantitative estimates of the G.S.P. trade benefits likely to accrue to the beneficiary developing countries. This, of course, is no easy task. The reader must bear in mind from the beginning that the results presented are only rough estimates.

Any *ex ante* evaluation that might be attempted runs into a number of insurmountable obstacles such as: (1) at the time of writing the single largest scheme – that of the United States – was just being introduced; (2) there is no way to accurately estimate *ex ante* the restrictive effects of the rules of origin or the discretionary administration of the ceiling systems of Japan (due to its new flexible administration provisions) and the E.E.C. (due to the less rigid ceilings of semi-sensitive and non-sensitive products); and (3) there is no way of accurately estimating *ex ante* the impact of the G.S.P. on investment incentives. To make matters worse, the data used for this evaluation, by and large, apply to periods prior to the introduction of the first preference scheme in 1971; thus G.S.P. tariff rates will not have had time to influence the commodity composition of trade between the beneficiaries and the donors. Nevertheless, the data presented and the conclusions drawn should be sufficiently rigorous to give the reader a relatively sound understanding of the implications of the G.S.P. for developing countries.

This evaluation will be conducted in several stages, starting from the major points made in Chapter 4 – that many products of current export interest to developing countries have been excluded from the G.S.P. First, an examination will be made of the impact of the safeguard measures on the G.S.P. product coverage to arrive at an 'effective' product coverage which includes only those products having 'opened-ended' trading opportunities under the G.S.P.

The next stage will estimate benefits accruing to beneficiary developing countries. These benefits are separated into two components: first, a tariff revenue transfer element (AID) for those products having 'closed-ended' ceilings, and second, a trade-expansion element (trade creation and trade diversion) for the other products. These estimates will, by necessity, be calculated on an *ex ante* basis; however, they will be cross-checked to the extent possible by some recent evidence published by the UNCTAD Secretariat on actual trade experience under the G.S.P. Finally, implications of these estimates on import displacement of donor-country production and employment will be explored.

As mentioned previously, the G.S.P. is a tariff policy that can be effective in stimulating developing-country exports of only those products subject to duty in the donor countries. Over one-half of donor-country imports from the developing countries are admitted free of duty. Further, the G.S.P. was envisaged from the beginning to be a policy to stimulate developing-country exports of manufactured products. The donors, by and large, have interpreted this to be manufactured industrial products; thus, in the main, agricultural and fishery products are excluded from the G.S.P. Finally, in order to protect domestic producer and worker groups, the donors have also excluded a number of 'import-sensitive' products of proven export interest to the developing countries. These three factors can only be expected to substantially limit the scope of the G.S.P.

Estimates of this scope have been calculated by the UNCTAD Secretariat using 1970 data provided by donor-country governments on computer tapes. The calculations involved accumulating each donor country's imports from all of its G.S.P. beneficiaries according to the duty treatment accorded each product group. Three accumulations were calculated: (1) total imports; (2) imports of products subject to duty under most-favoured-nation treatment of GATT; and (3) imports of products which are designated in the G.S.P. schemes. For each donor country, the beneficiary developing countries differ, the products subject to M.F.N. duties differ, and the products included in the G.S.P. differ. A summary of these calculations is presented in Table 7.1.

These data reveal that for all donors combined only 12 per cent of total beneficiary trade involves products which come under the various G.S.P. schemes. The reasons for this rather discouraging figure differ from donor to donor. For example, the schemes of Canada, Switzerland and New Zealand provide for G.S.P. tariff treatment on all industrial products subject to M.F.N. duty, yet on average cover only one-third of the imports of industrial products from the beneficiaries. This simply reflects the large share of industrial trade with developing countries that involves products admitted duty-free (i.e. industrial raw materials); in the industrial products' area these donors are doing all they can. Japan and Sweden are especially miserly in this regard as their industrial product coverage accounts for only 22 and 30 per cent of dutiable trade, respectively.

TABLE 7.1

*Donor-country imports from beneficiaries**

	Total imports	Dutiable imports	Covered by G.S.P.	G.S.P. as total	Share of dutiable
	(1970 in millions of $ U.S.)			(per cent)	(per cent)
E.E.C.	18175	5479	1447	8	26
Agricultural and fishery products	4683	3850	357	8	9
Industrial products	13492	1629	1090	8	67
United States	7846	4539	1712	22	38
Agricultural and fishery products	3421	1387	809	24	58
Industrial products	4425	3152	903	20	29
Japan	6906	3984	772	11	19
Agricultural and fishery products	1059	640	29	3	5
Industrial products	5847	3344	743	13	22
Canada	911	276	164	18	60
Agricultural and fishery products	242	133	21	9	16
Industrial products	669	143	143	21	100
Sweden	673	222	33	5	15
Agricultural and fishery products	223	134	7	3	5
Industrial products	450	88	26	6	30
Switzerland	491	288	185	38	64
Agricultural and fishery products	210	116	13	6	11
Industrial products	281	172	172	61	100
Austria	247	114	97	39	86
Agricultural and fishery products	95	58	48	51	83
Industrial products	152	56	49	32	88
Finland	200	110	5	3	5
Agricultural and fishery products	118	106	2	2	2
Industrial products	82	4	3	40	75
Norway	188	17	10	5	59
Agricultural and fishery products	85	11	6	7	55
Industrial products	103	6	4	4	67
New Zealand	142	31	28	20	90
Agricultural and fishery products	24	9	6	25	67
Industrial products	118	22	22	19	100
TOTAL	35779	15060	4453	12	30
AGRICULTURAL AND FISHERY PRODUCTS	10160	6444	1299	13	20
INDUSTRIAL PRODUCTS	25619	8616	3154	12	37

* The developing countries considered beneficiaries differ from donor to donor. Moreover, the E.E.C. grants more favourable tariff treatment to forty-six developing countries under the Lomé Convention; consequently these countries are not considered G.S.P. beneficiaries in these calculations.

Note: The product-group breakdown of total imports is according to the B.T.N. definitions of agricultural and fishery products included in chapters 1–24 and industrial products in chapters 25–99. The U.S. G.S.P. coverage for 1970 was estimated from 1973 trade flows and deflated to 1970 levels; these figures exclude trade with the newly designated beneficiaries – Cyprus, Hong Kong, Israel, Rumania, Somalia and Turkey.
SOURCE: UNCTAD Secretariat calculations, reported in documents *TD/B/C.5/22* and *TD/B/C.5/38*.

The United States is somewhat better but is still far from the 100 per cent category. However, in all fairness to these donors it must be pointed out that a substantial share of the non-covered industrial trade involves a single product – petroleum – which will retain its marketability regardless of G.S.P. tariff treatment. Petroleum alone accounts for over 90 per cent of the trade in industrial products excluded from Japan's G.S.P.; the corresponding figure for the United States is 28 per cent. If petroleum is ignored in calculating the G.S.P. product coverage for industrial products, the G.S.P. coverage rises to nearly 60 per cent of dutiable trade in industrial products. The remaining dutiable industrial products excluded from the G.S.P. are

TABLE 7.2

Product group	Value in $ millions	Share (per cent)*
All products	35779	100
less duty-free	−20719	58
less dutiable agricultural and fishery items not covered by G.S.P.	−5145	14
less dutiable petroleum items not covered by G.S.P.	−3065	9
less other dutiable industrial items not covered by G.S.P.		
textiles and footwear	−637	2
industrial raw materials	−591	2
import-sensitive electronic items excluded by the United States	−557	2
miscellaneous other items	−612	2
G.S.P. product coverage	4453	12

* Shares do not add to 100 due to rounding.

primarily textiles, footwear, industrial raw materials (other than petroleum) and import-sensitive electronic items excluded by the United States. These product breakdowns under the G.S.P. are summarised for all donor countries combined in Table 7.2. The end result is that the scope of the G.S.P. is limited to 12 per cent of donor-country imports from the beneficiary developing countries; yet the trade involved is nearly $4·5 billion annually based on 1970 trade-flow levels. Given the rapid growth in developing-country exports of manufactured products, the 1976 G.S.P. trade volume should be in the neighbourhood of $15 billion.*

* By 1973 U.S. imports of G.S.P. products had roughly doubled; E.E.C. G.S.P. trade doubled by 1972.

While the share of trade coming under the G.S.P. provisions might be considered small, the trade volume is not inconsequential and is growing rapidly. Since this earlier growth occurred without the stimulus of the G.S.P., the current question is: What contribution will the G.S.P. make to expand further beneficiary exports of manufactured products? The answer to this question obviously depends upon the price (or profit) incentives created by the preferential tariff reductions.

But in evaluating this question we must remember that the major schemes contain safeguard measures which limit the trade volume that will receive G.S.P. tariff treatment – administered on a product-by-product basis. The U.S. 'competitive-need' criteria eliminates G.S.P. tariff treatment on any product which the United States imports from a single beneficiary country in excess of (1) $25 million annually, or (2) 50 per cent of total U.S. imports of the product. Products which exceed either of these limits must, in effect, be considered as products not included in the U.S. G.S.P. for the particular beneficiaries concerned. By eliminating all such cases, from the G.S.P. pro-duct coverage calculated above we arrive at the 'effective product coverage' for the U.S. G.S.P.

Similarly, the schemes of the E.E.C. and Japan contain ceiling systems which limit the trade to receive G.S.P. tariff treatment. But unlike the U.S. 'competitive-need' criteria, the ceilings are re-opened at the beginning of each year. For these two schemes the question of export stimulation depends upon whether the G.S.P. tariff margins operate on expanded trade volumes. If the ceilings are inadequate to provide G.S.P. tariff treatment on trade flows in excess of that which would occur in the absence of the G.S.P., the preferential tariff rates will not provide any price incentive for expanded trade. In such cases, the only benefit accruing to developing countries will be the tariff revenue forgone by the donor on the ceiling level of trade. In the final analysis, then, the value of the G.S.P. in expanding trade depends upon the tariff margins which apply on expanded levels of trade. The margins will be zero when normal non-G.S.P. trade flows exceed the ceilings; the 'effec-tive product coverage' of these schemes should therefore exclude all pro-ducts which have 'closed-ended' ceilings.

Estimates of the adverse impact of these safeguards on G.S.P. trade in industrial products are presented in Table 7.3.* These figures reveal that over $1·7 billion in trade will be refused G.S.P. tariff treatment, thereby reducing the G.S.P. product coverage from $2·7 billion to an 'effective' coverage of only $1·0 billion. Moreover, the U.S. 'competitive-need' criteria eliminates G.S.P. tariff treatment on an additional $500 million in agricul-

---

* G.S.P. trade in agricultural and fishery products is excluded from these figures. The schemes of the E.E.C. and Japan do not apply ceiling limits to such trade, although normal non-tariff barriers to trade continue to operate. At this time the developing countries' G.S.P. trade advantages in the agricultural and fishery sectors are more a hope than an actuality, depending upon future improvements in the G.S.P. schemes rather than on existing provisions.

tural and fishery trade – mostly sugar. Thus in total the application of these ceiling-type safeguards reduces the effective product coverage of the G.S.P. by over $2 billion annually (out of a total product coverage under all ten G.S.P. schemes of $4·5 billion). What remains is a G.S.P. covering less than $2·5 billion in donor-country trade with the developing countries; this amounts to only 7 per cent of total donor–beneficiary trade.

TABLE 7.3

Effective coverage of industrial products
(1970 in millions of U.S. dollars)

	United States*	E.E.C.†	Japan
Total G.S.P. product coverage	903	1,090	743
G.S.P. trade affected by			
safeguard measures	−319	−737	−664
(1) $25 million limit (United States only)	(184)	—	—
(2) 50 per cent limit (United States only)	(135)	—	—
(3) ceiling limit (E.E.C. and Japan)	—	(351)	(615)
(4) maximum-amount limit (E.E.C. and Japan)	—	(263)	(49)
(5) allocation limit (E.E.C. only)	—	(123)	—
Effective G.S.P. product coverage	584	353	79
as share of total G.S.P. product			
coverage (per cent)	65	32	11
as share of trade in dutiable			
industrial products (per cent)	19	22	2

* Estimated from 1973 data and deflated to 1970 level.
† Estimated from 1969 data covering the original six E.E.C. member states. Calculations using 1972 data covering the enlarged E.E.C. of nine yield an 'effective product coverage' of $572 million out of $1625 million total G.S.P. coverage; the impact of the individual elements of the ceiling system could not be determined.
SOURCE: UNCTAD Secretariat calculations, reported in documents *TD/B/C.5/15*, *TD/B/C.5/38* and *TD/B/C.5/34*.

The division of G.S.P. trade among the beneficiary developing countries is extremely uneven, as indicated by the data presented in Table 7.4. The nine countries listed account for over two-thirds of the G.S.P. product coverage and over three-quarters of the effective G.S.P. trade. Thus even some relatively minor suppliers are adversely affected by the ceiling-type limits. Even though a concentration of trade could have been anticipated, the degree of the existing concentration is more than one would have expected. Taiwan alone accounts for almost 20 per cent of the effective G.S.P. trade even though it does not enjoy beneficiary status under one of the three major schemes (the E.E.C.'s). Over half of the effective G.S.P. trade is accounted for by only four of the more than one hundred beneficiary developing countries.

TABLE 7.4

Effective G.S.P. coverage and major suppliers of industrial products
(1970 in millions of U.S. dollars)

Beneficiary supplier	U.S. scheme*		E.E.C. scheme†		Japan scheme		Total	
	G.S.P. product	Effective coverage	G.S.P. product	Effective coverage	G.S.P. product	Effective coverage	G.S.P. product	Effective coverage
Taiwan	492	219	—	—	73	23	565	242
Mexico	400	175	21	15	11	9	432	199
Yugoslavia	42	40	356	111	1	1	399	152
South Korea	229	96	48	15	52	19	329	130
Hong Kong‡	—	—	254	23	—	—	254	23
Brazil	90	83	85	36	15	11	190	130
Singapore	127	50	34	12	7	3	168	65
India	45	37	38	18	61	9	144	64
Iran	—	—	104	22	0	0	104	22
Sub-total	1569	700	940	252	220	75	2585	1027
Other Beneficiaries	218	134	150	101	523	4	1035	239
TOTAL	1787	834	1090	353	743	79	3620	1266

* Calculated from 1973 data and deflated to 1970 trade levels. At the time these calculations were made, the final product coverage was not known; these figures include import-sensitive electronic and glass articles as well as a few other items subsequently removed from the U.S. G.S.P. The estimated product coverage, incorporating these new deletions, is $903 million. The 'effective' product coverage would be $584 million. The effect of these deletions on each country could not be determined from existing data.

† Calculated from 1972 data and deflated to 1970 trade levels.

‡ Hong Kong has since been added to the U.S. beneficiary list. Hong Kong is subject to special exclusions under Japan's scheme.

Note: — indicates that the developing country is not a beneficiary under the G.S.P. scheme.

SOURCE: UNCTAD Secretariat calculations, reported in documents *TD/B/C.5/15*, *TD/B/C.5/38* and *TD/B/C.5/34* (addendum 1).

TRADE BENEFITS UNDER THE G.S.P.[1]

The ultimate objective of the G.S.P. is to stimulate an increase in developing-country exports and export earnings, thereby providing resources and profit incentives for further industrialisation and more rapid economic growth. As mentioned earlier, the G.S.P. established preferential tariff margins in favour of donor-country imports originating in the beneficiary developing countries. These tariff margins create price incentives for donor-country importers (1) to increase the volume of their imports, and (2) to switch their source of supply from non-beneficiaries to beneficiaries. These two incentives are normally referred to as 'trade creation' and 'trade diversion', respectively.

But these incentives operate only when the G.S.P. tariff rates apply on expanded trade flows. For those cases in which the ceiling-type safeguards are operative – the ceilings are 'closed-ended' – the preferential tariff margins do not operate and there is no incentive for trade expansion. Such safeguards are extremely important under the U.S., E.E.C. and Japanese schemes. The U.S. G.S.P. completely eliminates G.S.P. tariff treatment on the affected products for the affected beneficiaries; however, the E.E.C. and Japanese schemes provide that the ceilings be re-opened at the beginning of each year. Thus under the latter two schemes there is the possibility of a resource transfer even though the incentive for trade expansion disappears. The resource-transfer possibility derives from the fact that the donor country does not assess duties on the ceiling levels of trade;* the forgone tariff revenue is therefore available to the importers. If the importers are highly competitive and must actively bid for beneficiary exports, this forgone tariff revenue would result in higher export prices and thus would accrue to the beneficiary exporters. On the other hand, if it is the beneficiary exporters who are highly competitive, facing monopsonistic donor-country importers in the E.E.C. and Japan, the forgone tariff revenue would remain in the hands of the importers; little, if any, benefit would be transferred to the beneficiary exporters.

Of course, what actually happens depends upon the relative market power of the importers and exporters. For some products the revenue transfer will occur; for others it will not; for still others, the forgone tariff revenue will be shared by the importers and exporters. But no matter how the tariff revenue is divided between importer and exporter, the share which accrues to the exporter does not stimulate expanded trade flows and thus cannot be considered the result of a 'trade' policy; instead it is considered 'aid'.

Any attempts to estimate this 'aid' benefit resulting from the G.S.P. schemes of the E.E.C. and Japan is extremely troublesome. First, it is necessary to identify all products which would be affected by the ceiling safeguard; this is very difficult because of the overlapping nature of the ceiling systems which contain (1) limits on G.S.P. imports from all beneficiaries combined, (2) limits on G.S.P. imports from individual beneficiaries, and (3) in the case of the E.E.C. limits on G.S.P. imports into each of the member states. The second problem involves calculating the tariff revenue forgone on the ceiling level of imports.† The third problem is by far the most difficult (and in all likelihood impossible) to solve with even a moderate degree of accuracy. This involves determining the actual sharing of the forgone tariff revenue between donor-country importers and developing-country exporters.

---

* This forgone tariff revenue could also be considered as a pseudo terms-of-trade improvement for the beneficiary exporter which applies only up to the ceiling level of trade (see pp. 67–9).
† The calculation simply requires multiplying the product ceiling level of trade by the M.F.N. tariff rate and accumulating across all products affected by the ceiling system. In cases where the maximum-amount limit is the only constraint, the M.F.N. duty is multiplied by this maximum-amount limit rather than the full ceiling level.

The first estimation problem has been overcome rather well in studies conducted by the UNCTAD Secretariat. The methodology involves comparing pre-G.S.P. trade flows with the ceiling, maximum-amount and allocation (for the E.E.C.) limits on a product-by-product basis. Using 1970 trade flows to identify 'closed-ended' products and post-Kennedy Round M.F.N. tariff rates, the forgone tariff revenue is estimated to be in the neighbourhood of $13 million under the E.E.C. G.S.P. and $14·5 million for Japan's G.S.P. The E.E.C. figure results from multiplying the 10·6 per cent unweighted average M.F.N. tariff rate for 'closed-ended' products by the $122 million ceiling or maximum-amount limit accounted for by these products. The Japanese revenue flow estimate is based on a 10 per cent average M.F.N. tariff. Thus the combined revenue estimates amount to roughly $27·5 million.

The final problem, as emphasised above, is that all this forgone tariff revenue does not go to beneficiary exporters. Unfortunately there is no evidence on which to base an estimate of the division of this revenue between donor importers and beneficiary exporters; hence we can only speculate as to how much 'aid' the latter will receive. However, we can confidently state that the exporters will receive less than the $27·5 million estimated above.* But of much more importance to the developing countries is the trade-expanding incentives.

The trade-expansion incentives operate through the preferential tariff reductions which enable importers to obtain certain goods at a lower landed cost if such imports originate in a beneficiary developing country. This provides two price incentives.

(1) The importer gains a new price competitiveness over domestic producers of similar import-competing products. The importer can, as a result of this tariff saving, lower his price to consumers, who would then buy more, the importer can offer special discounts to retailers or wholesalers, who would then increase their selling efforts, or the importer can increase his advertising or other product-promotion efforts to attract increased buyer attention. In any of these ways the importer can use the tariff saving to increase his share of the domestic market. This effect is commonly referred to as 'trade creation' – increased imports resulting from a combination of increased consumer purchases and decreased domestic production.

(2) Since the tariff saving comes only when imports originate in a beneficiary country, importers have an incentive to substitute imports from beneficiaries for imports from other sources, i.e. non-beneficiaries. This is commonly referred to as 'trade diversion' – increased imports from beneficiaries resulting from decreased imports from non-beneficiaries.

---

* Of course this conclusion applies only to 1970 ceiling levels. By 1975, normal trade growth would result in additional products facing 'closed-ended' ceilings. A crude estimate of the maximum forgone tariff revenue would be $50 million.

The methodology for estimating such trade-creation and trade-diversion impacts has been well developed and refined in numerous recent studies of the trade effects resulting from the creation of customs unions (primarily the E.E.C.) and free-trade areas (primarily the European Free Trade Area – EFTA).[2] These studies have generally concentrated on the welfare impact of a consumer benefit – as consumers obtain lower-priced goods – and a world resource saving – as goods are produced under lower-cost conditions. In this terminology, trade creation benefits world welfare as consumers benefit from lower-priced imports and more goods are produced using cheaper foreign resources, thereby saving more expensive domestic resources. Conversely, trade diversion reduces world welfare because the preferential tariff treatment causes a substitution of higher resource cost imports from the customs union or free-trade area partner for lower resource cost imports from other sources*.

The evaluation of the G.S.P., however, concentrates on different interpretations of the concepts of trade creation and trade diversion. In the first place, world welfare is of little concern; the G.S.P. aims at increasing developing-country welfare and is only incidentally concerned with donor-country consumers or non-beneficiary exporters. The central concern is the increase in exports of the developing countries. Beneficiary exports increase from trade-creation and trade-diversion incentives; thus both concepts operate in favour of the developing countries.

Second, the traditional trade-creation and trade-diversion concepts emphasise the welfare gain, i.e. the marginal resource saving as resources are reallocated from a relatively inefficient use to a marginally more efficient employment. This is the proper evaluation in cases where the full employment of a nation's resources is maintained. However, in the case of the G.S.P., it seems appropriate to consider the resulting trade expansion to involve a movement to a higher level of utilisation of the beneficiary nation's resources. Furthermore, the trade expansion generates a higher level of foreign-exchange earnings which is a significant benefit in its own right. For these two reasons, the trade benefits of the G.S.P. will be estimated as the total of trade creation and trade diversion rather than through the traditional net change in welfare concept.

Trade creation is traditionally estimated using import demand elasticities:

$$TC_i = M_i e_i[dt_i/(1 + t_i)], \tag{7.1}$$

where TC is the trade creation, M the initial level of donor-country imports from beneficiaries, e the import demand elasticity, dt the change in the tariff rate (in this case the preferential tariff margin which equals the M.F.N. tariff rate) t the initial M.F.N. tariff rate, and the subscript i denotes the particular product.

* These general welfare considerations are discussed in more detail in Chapter 2, pp. 21–3.

Trade diversion is much more difficult to estimate; it is a substitution effect as importers substitute imports from beneficiaries for imports from non-beneficiaries. Theoretically, such estimates require *a priori* knowledge about the magnitude of substitution elasticities. Such elasticities are simply not available, especially for disaggregated product groups. Hence an alternative method is required to estimate trade diversion.

One starting point for an alternative estimation technique would be to note that the non-beneficiary countries are, by and large, developed countries which are also donor countries, i.e. the United States and Japan are non-beneficiaries for the E.E.C. scheme, the E.E.C. and Japan are non-beneficiaries for the U.S. scheme, and so on. For this reason it seems reasonable to assume that the substitutability between a beneficiary export product and a similar product produced in a non-beneficiary country would be similar to the substitutability between a beneficiary export product and a similar product produced in the donor country. Thus the loss of sales by non-beneficiary exporters would be proportional to the loss of sales by donor-country domestic producers. Since this latter loss is trade creation, the former loss (trade diversion) becomes:

$$TD_i = TC_i(Mn_i/V_i), \tag{7.2}$$

where TD is trade diversion; Mn is donor imports from non-beneficiary sources, and V is donor-country production.

The trade-expansion components were estimated on an annual 1970 trade-flow basis using 1971 data for four-digit Brussels Tariff Nomenclature (B.T.N.) product categories. In order to simplify the calculations, samples of product categories were selected which include all products in which imports from all developing countries (not just beneficiaries) exceeded $500,000 for the United States or $1 million for the E.E.C. and Japan. These samples cover, respectively, 98, 85 and 97 per cent of total exports from developing countries into the United States, the E.E.C. and Japan. The sample values were then extrapolated to estimate the trade creation and trade diversion that would apply to the actual 1970 G.S.P. imports from beneficiaries, as shown in the first column of Table 7.5. The figures for the other donors were assumed to be proportional to the average percentage increase in beneficiary exports to the United States, the E.E.C. and Japan. The import demand price elasticities which were used apply to the United States only; elasticity estimates for the other donors were not available at the degree of product disagregation used in these calculations.[3] The trade-diversion figures were estimated using sub-samples which include only those products having an estimated trade creation of more than $500,000. This simplification covered over 90 per cent of the total trade-creation. The ratios of non-beneficiary imports to domestic production were calculated for each product in these sub-samples.[4] For the remaining products, the median ratios for all items in each sub-sample were used; the median ratios are 7 per

TABLE 7.5

Trade benefits of G.S.P.
(1970 in millions of U.S. dollars)

| | | G.S.P. trade expansion | | |
Donor	Imports of G.S.P. products	Trade creation	Trade diversion	Total
Trade expansion excluding products with 'closed-ended' ceilings				
United States	584	136	33	169
E.E.C.*	353	82	7	89
Japan†	79	22	1	23
Other donors‡	418	98	15	113
Total	1434	338	56	394
Trade expansion without ceiling-type safeguards				
United States	903	192	41	233
E.E.C.	1090	278	25	303
Japan	333	70	2	72
Other donors	418	98	15	113
Total	3154	638	83	721

* A number of beneficiary countries in Africa, the Caribbean and the Pacific have more favourable access to E.E.C. markets under the Lomé Convention association agreement and therefore do not really benefit from the E.E.C. G.S.P. scheme. These countries have been excluded from the E.E.C. calculations.

† Copper has been excluded because of its unusual M.F.N. duty – the tariff ranges from zero to roughly 7 per cent *ad valorem* depending upon the world price of copper. Copper is included in the Japanese G.S.P. but was initially assigned a 'zero' ceiling because it was duty-free in 1968 and 1969 – the base years used to calculate the ceiling.

‡ The trade-creation and trade-diversion figures were estimated to be equal to the average percentage increase in beneficiary exports to the United States, the E.E.C. and Japan. Since the other donors do not have ceiling-type safeguards, these estimates are not affected by 'closed-ended' ceilings.

SOURCE: Robert E. Baldwin and Tracy Murray, 'M.F.N. Tariff Reductions and Developing Country Trade Benefits Under the G.S.P.', *Economic Journal*, March 1977.

cent for the United States, 3 per cent for the E.E.C. and 3 per cent for Japan.

The estimated trade-expansion figures were presented in Table 7.5. These calculations do not take account of trade that did not exist prior to the G.S.P. but might be created by the preferential tariff reductions. Such an omission tends to bias the estimates downwards; it is unlikely, however, that this bias is very large. The first set of estimates are based on the institutional provisions of the G.S.P. as it currently operates. The total estimated trade expansion is in the neighbourhood of $400 million; this represents a 27 per cent increase from the 1970 trade flow of $1·4 billion. The bulk of this increase is due to trade creation, i.e. increased consumer purchases (because of the lower price) and decreased domestic production. This finding is consistent with results of other empirical studies of trade creation and trade diversion in the more traditional context of customs unions and free-trade areas.

The second set of estimates presented in Table 7.5 represents the trade expansion that would occur if the ceiling-type safeguards did not exist, i.e. the ceiling systems of the E.E.C. and Japan and the 'competitive-need' criteria of the United States. The effective trade-flow coverage would more than double from $1·4 billion to $3·2 billion. The total trade expansion would increase to over $700 million, an 83 per cent increase. Put somewhat differently, the ceiling-type safeguards cost the beneficiaries over $300 million in forgone annual trade expansion.

In summary, the G.S.P. as it currently exists provides a trade-expansion benefit for industrial products estimated to be in the neighbourhood of $400 million annually. In addition, the E.E.C. and Japan forgo $27·5 million in tariff revenue on those products for which imports exceed ceiling, maximum amount of ceiling allocation limits; this transfer is divided between donor importers and beneficiary exporters depending upon their respective market power. Assuming all of this $27·5 million actually accrues to the beneficiaries, the total industrial product 'trade plus aid' benefit for the beneficiary developing countries amounts to some $425 million. This annual trade benefit amounts to 13 per cent of the $3·2 billion 1970 trade flow in G.S.P. products – 5 per cent of donor imports of dutiable industrial products or less than 2 per cent of total donor imports of industrial products.

The trade benefits accruing on agricultural and fishery products have not been carefully estimated because of the numerous non-tariff barriers affecting such trade. The only G.S.P. safeguard measure that applies on agricultural and fishery product trade is the U.S. 'competitive-need' criteria and, of course, the rather liberal escape clause.* Unfortunately, the U.S. 'competitive-need' criteria eliminates G.S.P. tariff treatment on just over two-thirds of U.S. G.S.P. imports. Thus the 'effective' G.S.P. agricultural and fishery sector product coverage is reduced from $1·3 billion to $750 million. Starting from this base, a trade expansion much in excess of $100 million would be highly unlikely.† Such a trade benefit would amount to less than 2 per cent of donor-country imports of dutiable agricultural and fishery products.

Thus, upon combining the 'trade plus aid' benefit from industrial products and the $100 million estimate from agricultural and fishery products, the total benefit to all beneficiary developing countries accruing under all G.S.P.

---

* The ceiling systems of the E.E.C. and Japan apply only to the G.S.P. trade in industrial products.

† In fact, a $50 million figure might be much closer since G.S.P. tariff rates on agricultural and fishery products are often far above the G.S.P. duty-free status of most industrial products.

schemes is estimated to be roughly $500–600 million. Thus this preferential
tariff policy stimulates an estimated 4 per cent increase in trade subject to
M.F.N. duties – 1·5 per cent of total donor–beneficiary trade.

IMPACT ON DONOR-COUNTRY PRODUCTION AND EMPLOYMENT

The primary purpose of the G.S.P. is to stimulate an increase in developing-
country exports and export earnings. The donor countries, however, were
very concerned that such an increase in imports would adversely affect
domestic producers and workers. It was to guard against the potential
'flood' of preferential imports that ceiling-type safeguard measures were
introduced into the G.S.P. schemes of the United States, the E.E.C. and
Japan. The previous section demonstrated that these restrictive effects cut
the trade benefits of the G.S.P. roughly in half. But does the potential
import-displacement injury to domestic producers and workers justify such
restrictive safeguard measures? Remember that the ceiling-type safeguards
are all automatic and become operative even when there is no causal relationship between G.S.P. imports and injury to domestic industries. It is this
lack of causal tie that has led to the repeated criticisms that the safeguard
measures are unjustifiably restrictive.

However, it must be noted that this previous criticism and, in fact, nearly
all earlier analyses of the G.S.P. have been motivated by a concern for the
trade benefits of the beneficiary developing countries. Almost no concern
has been directed towards the impact of the G.S.P. on the donor countries.
But if the G.S.P. is really as effective as people hope it will be, beneficiary
exports of non-traditional manufactured products will increase substantially. And this increased trade cannot help but adversely affect the production of G.S.P. products in the donor countries. Donor-country producers
will suffer on two accounts: (1) decreased sales to domestic consumers, who
substitute lower-priced imports from beneficiaries for domestic output; and
(2) decreased exports to other donors, who substitute lower-priced imports
from beneficiaries for imports from non-beneficiaries, mainly other donors.
These two effects are the same trade effects estimated earlier as trade creation and trade diversion, respectively*.

There are a number of problems in estimating the production and employment impacts even if accurate estimates of trade creation and trade
diversion are available. First, trade creation consists of two components: (1)
an increase in consumption of the lower-priced good; and (2) a reduction in
domestic sales of domestically produced goods. The latter component results from a substitution of imports for domestic production and, therefore,

---

* The trade-diversion effect on production and employment of, say, the United States is that
share of other donors' trade diversion (say of the E.E.C. Japan, and so on) which is accounted
for by the United States.

adversely affects domestic production and employment. However, the former represents an *increase* in consumption due to the new lower price and does not reflect a lower level of domestic production. Empirically, these two elements cannot be separated. Thus our estimates of the import displacement of domestic production and employment, which are based on trade creation, will overstate this element of the adverse effect of the G.S.P. on donor-country producers and workers.

The second difficulty stems from the fact that domestic production and employment impacts normally consist of two levels of impact – the direct and indirect effects. The direct effects are simply the loss in sales of domestically produced output as measured by trade creation and trade diversion. These direct effects can be estimated quite easily using input–output coefficients. The indirect effects refer to the loss of sales by secondary domestic producers who supply inputs to those firms experiencing the adverse direct effects. In addition, there are the aggregate income effects as reduced employment causes a decline in national income, reducing the level of aggregate spending and causing secondary declines in sales, production and employment in unrelated consumer-goods industries all across the nation. If these latter secondary effects prove to be troublesome, the corrective measures usually take the form of national economic policy initiatives such as expansionary monetary or fiscal policy. Moreover, any such secondary effects would probably be lost among the multitude of purely domestic adjustments which normally affect the industrial nations – adjustments caused by such factors as technological innovation, increased population, normal variations in weather affecting agricultural output, as well as outdoor production such as construction, mining, fishing, and so on. Because of such problems in identifying the indirect effects, the estimated G.S.P. impact on donor-country production and employment will be based on the direct effects alone*.

The estimates are presented in Table 7.6 and are based upon the earlier estimates of trade creation and trade diversion (given in Table 7.5). For all donors combined the adverse production effect is estimated to be roughly $400 million for industrial products; the adverse direct employment effect is less than 25,000 jobs. To put the production effect in its proper perspective it is only necessary to mention that the production of manufactured products by the donor countries is measured in hundreds of billions of U.S. dollars whereas the G.S.P. impact is measured in hundreds of millions. Thus, at most, the production effect would amount to a very small fraction of 1 per cent of domestic production.

---

* A further justification for ignoring the indirect effects would be that the increased export earnings of the beneficiaries would in all likelihood be re-spent in the same donor countries, thereby maintaining aggregate demand for total output and employment – though the composition of aggregate demand may change somewhat.

TABLE 7.6

Donor-country production and employment impacts of G.S.P. trade in industrial products

Donor	Employment (1969 jobs)	G.S.P. effects*				Normal change in employment†	
		Import displacement ($ m.)	Export displacement ($ m.)	Production displacement ($ m.)	G.S.P. job displacement (jobs)	Total (jobs)	Manufacturing (jobs)
United States	77,902,000	136	5	141	5217	1,426,000	650,000
E.E.C.	98,647,000	82	32	114	9550	−43,000	25,000
Japan	50,420,000	22	7	29	3057	733,000	595,000
Other donors	25,682,000	98	12	110	6586	219,000	159,000
Total	252,651,000	338	56	394	24,410	2,335,000	1,429,000

* The import displacement is simply trade creation; export displacement is that share of other donors' trade diversion which is accounted for by the particular donor(s).

† The normal employment changes are the average annual changes which occurred during 1965–9. These figures do not take into consideration normal relocations which occur in the labour force as some workers voluntarily leave their jobs, presumably to take better jobs elsewhere. In the United States this annual 'quit rate' is roughly 2·5 per cent of total manufacturing employment.

SOURCE: J. M. Finger, 'The Generalized Scheme of Preferences – Impact on the Donor Countries', *Bulletin of Economic Research*, May 1973; and Table 7.5.

To place the direct employment effect in context, data on total employment and changes in employment are also presented in Table 7.6. In comparison with the total employment of some 250 million, the G.S.P. impact of 25,000 jobs seems inconsequential. Moreover, when compared with the normal changes in the level of employment of 1·4 million jobs in manufacturing alone, the G.S.P. impact appears to be well within a magnitude that can be readily absorbed by the normal growth in employment opportunities; and note that this normal growth in job opportunities excludes the even larger normal adjustments which the labour force makes to changing economic conditions – mostly initiated by domestic events alone. For example, during the 1965–9 period there was an annual exodus of workers from the agricultural sector of 1·6 million workers, workers which were re-absorbed in the industrial and services sectors. Thus in the aggregate the 25,000 workers affected by the G.S.P. should pose only minor re-absorption problems. In fact, even if the G.S.P. were liberalised by the elimination of all ceiling-type safeguards, the employment effect would be less than 50,000 workers – again a figure that could easily be re-absorbed in the donor-country labour markets.

This conclusion regarding the incidental aggregate production and employment effects should not, however, be generalised to each manufacturing industry or to each regional or skill-class labour market. In fact, we should suspect that certain industries or worker groups would be seriously affected by the G.S.P.; and the particular industries or workers affected may vary from donor to donor. But in the main the criticism of the non-causal automatic ceiling-type safeguard remains; it is obviously much more restrictive than necessary to safeguard the production and employment interests of the donor countries. The elimination of such safeguards would roughly double the trade benefits of the G.S.P. for the beneficiary developing countries without seriously affecting the donor countries. In those cases where particular producers or workers were seriously injured (or threatened with injury), a more narrowly defined safeguard would seem appropriate – a safeguard based on a causal tie between increased G.S.P. imports and injury to the particular domestic industry.

CONCLUSIONS AND ADDITIONAL QUALIFICATIONS

The overriding conclusion of this evaluation of the G.S.P. is rather depressing. Based on 1970 trade-flow levels, the G.S.P. as it is currently administered generates a trade-expansion benefit to the developing countries in the neighbourhood of only half a billion U.S. dollars annually; this is certainly not much when compared with the annual $35 billion plus trade between beneficiary exporters and donor importers. Even if the G.S.P. were to be liberalised by the elimination of the ceiling-type safeguards, the trade-expansion benefit would not significantly exceed $1 million annually. And finally, rather than a programme to help all developing countries, the vast majority of these trade benefits accrue to only a dozen or so developing countries (of the 150 or so designated as G.S.P. beneficiaries). The others have little opportunity or capacity to benefit substantially from any trade policy, let alone the very restrictive G.S.P.

On the more promising side, there have been serious negotiations aimed at improving the G.S.P. schemes of the various donors. Unfortunately, however, such progress has often been accompanied by increased restrictions imposed against the major beneficiary suppliers, for example in the form of smaller maximum-amount limits under the schemes of the E.E.C. and Japan. Thus those beneficiaries that are able to take advantage of a trade policy are being increasingly hindered in their efforts to do so. Moreover, over time the ceiling levels and comparative-need limits will increasingly come into play to further reduce their ability to benefit from the G.S.P.

This rather depressing conclusion must be further qualified to the extent that other elements limit beneficiary exporters access to donor markets. Two additional items come to mind. First, the estimates contained in this chapter have completely ignored the restrictive elements contained in the G.S.P. rules of origin. It would be impossible to accurately estimate such an impact. However, early experience under Japan's G.S.P. scheme revealed that approximately one-quarter of the trade in G.S.P. products not affected by any ceiling or maximum-amount limit did not receive G.S.P. tariff treatment. While it is doubtful that this substantial failure to receive G.S.P. tariff treatment is fully due to restrictive elements contained in the rules of origin, the rules of origin are without doubt a significant factor. There is also suspicion that a similar order of magnitude would apply under the schemes of the E.E.C. and the other European donors.

Second, the analysis ignores the impact of the numerous non-tariff barriers to trade which are completely unrelated to the G.S.P. – such non-tariff restrictions as contained in the health and safety standards, packaging and labelling regulations, credit restrictions, market controls, technical regulations, subsidies to import competitors, discriminatory governmental procurement practices, the variable levy system of the E.E.C., the voluntary export restrictions against trade in textiles, and so on.[5] The G.S.P. provides for a reduction in the tariff charged on a preferential basis; it does not provide for the relaxation of any other regulation governing international trade. There is some evidence of a general nature indicating that non-tariff barriers to trade do not seriously limit G.S.P. trade.[6] However, this evidence did not contain a product-by-product examination. There can be little doubt that E.E.C. preferences for textile products are completely frustrated by the voluntary export restrictions imposed under the L.T.A. – recall that only those developing countries that abide by the L.T.A. are granted beneficiary status by the E.E.C. for textile products (see Chapter 4). Also E.E.C. preferences on agricultural products covered by the Common Agricultural Policy are of minimal value since the variable levy which operates to protect domestic producers is not reduced under the G.S.P. These examples were not chosen to pick on the E.E.C. but rather to indicate that for some products non-tariff barriers pose a more serious barrier to trade than M.F.N. tariff rates. Undoubtedly, the developing-country exporters will face similar problems in exporting under the G.S.P. provisions of other donors as well.

Finally, other events unrelated to the G.S.P. are simultaneously taking place which modify the rules governing international trade. In so doing, such events cannot help but influence the G.S.P. as well. Such events might include the recent 'oil crisis' and the collapse of the Bretton Woods system of international finance. Other events which have a much more direct impact on the G.S.P. are the recent enlargement of the E.E.C. from six to nine member states and the recently initiated Tokyo Round of multilateral tariff and non-tariff barrier negotiations under the auspices of GATT. Such events are the subject of Part 3.

PART 3

Other Issues Related to the G.S.P.

Introduction to Part 3

The G.S.P. was negotiated and introduced during a period of rapid change in the international economy. The E.E.C. was enlarged. World-wide inflation and recession brought with it a collapse of the international monetary system. The oil and food crises have brought further pressures on the international economy. Each of these events by itself would have substantial effects on the developing countries, but together their impact is certain to be enormous.

Part 3 considers the impact of such events on the G.S.P. Chapter 8 deals with the enlargement of the E.E.C., which has several impacts. First, this required a modification in the E.E.C.'s arrangements with the African Associates, the Commonwealth developing countries and the countries around the Mediterranean. The new arrangements provide numerous developing countries with special access to European markets which is more favourable than the access provided under the G.S.P. This has obvious implications for the value of the G.S.P. to the other developing countries. And second, the E.E.C. has negotiated a series of free-trade agreements with the remaining countries of Western Europe which, in effect, create a new West European free-trade area which will be fully implemented in 1977.

Chapter 9 examines the impact of the GATT trade negotiations on the G.S.P. Since any reduction in M.F.N. tariff rates reduces the preferential margins provided under the G.S.P., the developing countries are fearful that this GATT round will erode the value of the G.S.P. This erosion is compared with the offsetting benefits of lower M.F.N. tariffs; developing-country fears will prove to be well-founded only if the G.S.P. is improved by the complete elimination of the ceiling-type safeguards.

Chapter 10 attempts to identify the place of the G.S.P. in the 'new international economic order'. After summarising the value of the G.S.P. as it exists today, it is suggested that prospects for meaningful improvements are dim. However, alternative measures to promote manufactured exports are promising. The new emphasis on commodities is questioned and, finally, we look at the question: North–South relations, confrontation or co-operation?

8

The Evolving Trade Relations of the E.E.C.

At the time the G.S.P. was being negotiated international trade was 'considered' to be governed by the most-favoured-nation (M.F.N.) principle of GATT. However, in reality there were a number of preferential arrangements in operation, for example the European Customs Union (E.E.C.), the European Free Trade Area (EFTA), the British Commonwealth Area, and the E.E.C. association agreement with eighteen African countries (Yaoundé Convention). Each of these exceptions to the M.N.F. principle provided for preferential tariff treatment on a reciprocal basis. In essence each party to an agreement discriminated against imports from third countries and in favour of imports from other members of its respective agreement. Thus the Commonwealth developing countries discriminated in favour of U.K. exports and received preferential access for their exports in U.K. markets; similarly the African states associated with the E.E.C. granted special access to E.E.C. exports and received special access to E.E.C. markets. The major tool of discrimination was preferential tariff rates.

As a consequence, there is a hierarchy of access to a particular market – most preferred are domestic producers who face no import barriers; second come the preferred trading partners who face reduced import barriers but must comply with rules of origin; third come GATT trading partners who receive general M.F.N. treatment; and finally come those non-GATT partners who are discriminated against, generally socialist countries of Eastern Europe and China.

The advantage of preferred access is that importers have an incentive to purchase imports from the preferred sources since such imports will be charged lower import taxes than if they originated in a non-preferred country; and thus the value of preferred access depends upon the extent to which a preferred country's products compete with products from non-preferred sources. If there are no non-preferred sources, or if the non-preferred countries do not export competitive products, preferred access has very little value. This point is central to the value of the G.S.P. schemes granted by the European donors due to the interlocking maze of preferential trading arrangements that have been and are being created in the aftermath of the enlargement of the E.E.C.

At the time the E.E.C. introduced the first G.S.P. scheme in 1971, its membership consisted of six member states, namely Belgium, France, West Germany, Italy, Luxembourg and the Netherlands. Later, as a result of the Treaty of Accession signed in 1972, Denmark, Ireland and the United Kingdom joined. Such an act affected not only the trading relations between the joiners and the original six, it also affected the trading relations between each of these groups and the groups of developing countries tied to the original E.E.C. and the United Kingdom through trade agreements. In effect, these trading relations had to be completely restructured.

In the main the initial arrangements with the developing countries were a logical outgrowth of the post-colonial era during which a number of formerly dependent territories gained their political independence. But of course political independence and economic independence are not the same thing. In fact, in the majority of these cases the newly independent nations were very dependent on the former colonial powers for their economic livelihood. Much of their industrial capacity was owned and managed by colonial firms, and much of their foreign-exchange earnings depended upon the sales and marketing outlets of these now foreign-owned firms. It was very much in the interest of the newly independent nations to enter into agreements with their former colonial powers to provide a transitional 'phasing in' of their economic independence. These new governments had enough trouble stabilising their political environment to contend with any economic instability that must obviously result when economic control is transferred from one party to another.

The interest of the colonial power in perpetuating a relationship with the old colonies was also strong, economically as well as politically. Obviously, it wanted to continue to receive the flow of profits from firms which were operating in these countries as well as the flow of raw materials originating there; and political influence, once gained, is only grudgingly given up. Thus it was in the mutual interest of both the newly independent developing countries and the old colonial powers to formalise trading relationships through negotiated agreements.

SPECIAL ARRANGEMENTS PREDATING THE G.S.P.

Subsequent to the Treaty of Rome, which created the European Customs Union in 1957, the E.E.C. formalised arrangements with those developing countries and territories having historical ties with the member states under the Yaoundé Convention. In addition, arrangements were negotiated with a number of other developing countries in Africa and around the Mediterranean. These arrangements will be discussed in turn.

Yaoundé Convention

Under the Treaty of Rome, the E.E.C. of six agreed to an economic association with eighteen developing countries which had special post-colonial relations with Belgium, France, Italy and the Netherlands.* The initial

* The eighteen African Associates were Burundi, Cameroon, Central African Republic, Chad, Congo, Gabon, Dahomey, Ivory Coast, Madagascar, Mali, Mauritania, Niger, Rwanda, Senegal, Somalia, Togo, Upper Volta and Zaire.

agreement (signed in 1963) had a duration of five years, after which a new Convention was signed in 1969 and came into effect on 1 January 1971.* Under this agreement the associated African states would receive economic aid from the E.E.C. of up to nearly $1 billion in grants and loans through the European Development Fund and the European Investment Bank. Equally important were the provisions for preferential trading between the parties, i.e. African Associate exports to the E.E.C. receive preferential access as do E.E.C. exports to the African Associates. The E.E.C. granted unrestricted duty-free entry for imports from the Associates for all industrial products and for those agricultural products not covered by the Common Agricultural Policy (C.A.P.). For C.A.P. products, the Associates were exempt from a part of the import duty, generally the fixed duty element, and were to pay all (or in some cases only part) of the variable levy. In return the Associates granted preferential tariff or non-tariff treatment on imports from the E.E.C. It is clear that the Associates received more favourable access to E.E.C. markets than they granted to the E.E.C. in return; but even so the Yaoundé Convention was a mutual-interest agreement negotiated on a reciprocal basis. The E.E.C. gains a long-term promise of good relations with the African Associates; and the E.E.C. will go to many extremes to maintain and improve these relations.

Arusha Agreement

The Arusha Agreement (which became effective in 1971) provided for an association between the E.E.C. and the three countries of the East African Community (Kenya, Tanzania and Uganda, which continued to maintain their status as members of the British Commonwealth).† The objective of this agreement was to promote an increased flow of trade between the E.E.C. and East Africa; unlike the Yaoundé Convention there was no provision for economic aid.

The agreement provided duty-free access to E.E.C. markets for East African exports of all industrial products and some agricultural products – excluding those agricultural products covered by the C.A.P. as well as those products subject to quotas or other non-tariff measures of import protection. However, ceiling limits were imposed by the E.E.C. on preferential imports of certain tropical agricultural products. In return, the East African countries granted 'reverse' preferences ranging from 2 to 9 percentage points of *ad valorem* tariff rate in favour of E.E.C. exports of about sixty products.

For the vast majority of industrial products the advantages under the Arusha Agreement were on par with those under the Yaoundé Convention. However, the restrictions and exclusions for agricultural products under the

---

* Subsequently, Mauritius concluded an agreement with the E.E.C. (1972) and acceeded to the second Yaoundé Convention.
† The E.E.C. also concluded and signed an association agreement with Nigeria in 1966, but it was not ratified by Nigeria because of French support for Biafra.

Arusha Agreement were generally imposed to safeguard the trading interests of the Yaoundé countries. The final distinction that favours Yaoundé countries over Arusha countries was the aid element provided under the Yaoundé Convention but absent from the Arusha Agreement.

Mediterranean countries

Starting even before 1962, the E.E.C. was evolving a so-called 'Mediterranean policy' consisting of a number of co-operative trade agreements with the countries of the Mediterranean basin. This policy is designed to increase E.E.C. economic links with countries of the region, thereby increasing economic interdependence and leading to a political influence in the area not requiring the E.E.C. to become involved in international political disputes among these countries or domestic political disputes within them.

The first such agreements were negotiated with Greece (1962) and Turkey (1964). These two agreements were entered into in accordance with the most-favoured-nation principle of GATT as they ultimately provided for full membership in the European Customs Union – once the levels of economic development of the two 'joiners' catch up with that of the original six members of the E.E.C. Thus the agreements provided rather long periods (from twelve to twenty-two years) for staging the removal of intra-trade tariff barriers.

Under the Treaty of Rome the E.E.C. anticipated association agreements with Morocco and Tunisia, eventually signed in 1969. Under these agreements the E.E.C. grants duty-free access on imports of virtually all industrial products (excepting cork and articles of cork) originating in these two North African countries; substantial preferences are granted on a number of agricultural products as well. But as is the case under the other association agreements, preferential agricultural imports are often subject to ceiling limitations (in these agreements industrial petroleum products are also subject to certain limitations). In return Morocco and Tunisia grant tariff and quota concessions on many products of interest to the E.E.C. Morocco has, however, extended the tariff reductions to all GATT members on a most-favoured-nation basis.

The E.E.C. has also negotiated two-stage agreements with Malta (1971) and Cyprus (1972) which are envisaged to culminate in a free-trade area by the end of the second five-year stage. During the first stage, the E.E.C. agrees to reduce its duties on imports from the E.E.C. until E.E.C. exports receive treatment equal to U.K. exports under the Commonwealth Preferential Agreement.* Cyprus will also enjoy the 70 per cent duty reduction on its exports of all industrial products and preferential treatment on certain agricultural items. Cyprus will stage-in preferential duty reductions in favour of E.E.C. exports starting with a 15 per cent reduction which increases to 25 per

---

* Note that this agreement was enacted prior to the U.K. accession to the E.E.C.

cent after two years and reaches 35 per cent at the beginning of the fifth year.

Finally, the E.E.C. also negotiated separate trade agreements with Spain, Israel, Egypt and Lebanon. These agreements provide for preferential duty reductions on selected industrial and agricultural products introduced by both the signatories and the E.E.C. The terms of these agreements are subject to renegotiation and must be altered as a result of the enlargement of the E.E.C. from six to nine members. Although there might be intentions on the part of these Mediterranean countries to eventually become members of the E.E.C., transitional arrangements to this objective were not part of the initial agreements. In this sense these agreements do violate the non-discriminatory spirit of GATT.

Just recently (reported 19 January 1976) the E.E.C. has completed negotiations on trade and financial aid accords with Algeria as well as renewed agreements with Morocco and Tunisia. In addition, the E.E.C. announced that talks on similar treaties with Syria and Jordan are to start in the near future; Egypt's agreement is also scheduled for renegotiation. These recent initiatives result from a desire by the E.E.C. to improve its ties with the Arab world by revising the diplomatic imbalance caused by the recent signing of a trade treaty with Israel.

This, then, represents the complex of relations which the E.E.C. was in the process of establishing as the G.S.P. negotiations progressed. The Yaoundé Convention and the agreements with Greece and Turkey were already in force when the G.S.P. idea was first seriously introduced at the initial UNCTAD conference which convened in Geneva in 1964. By the time the G.S.P. was first taken seriously at the second UNCTAD conference in 1968, the Arusha, Morocco and Tunisia agreements were in the latter stages of negotiation. It is not surprising then that the E.E.C. was more concerned with successful association agreements than a worth-while G.S.P.

The Associates were concerned that their preferential access to E.E.C. markets would be jeopardised if all other developing countries received similar duty-free access under the G.S.P. In this case the value of their association status would be zero – even negative as they would be granting 'reverse' concessions to E.E.C. exports while receiving only what they could obtain on a non-reciprocal basis as a result of the G.S.P. Moreover, since many of these countries already enjoyed special access to E.E.C. markets, they feared that their exports to the E.E.C. would decline because of the increased competition from other beneficiary developing countries. Consequently, the Associates' position at the G.S.P. negotiations was somewhat contradictory – they favoured the introduction of very liberal G.S.P. schemes by the United States, Japan and the other European countries, while urging the E.E.C. to be particularly stingy concerning preferential treatment on products of export interest to them. The E.E.C. found itself in the uncomfortable position of having to reconcile the conflict of appeasing all developing countries while protecting the trading interests of the African Associates. The E.E.C. resolved this conflict by excluding industrial raw materials and agricultural commodities from its G.S.P. scheme while granting G.S.P. treatment on all manufactured and semi-manufactured industrial products. As was noted earlier, the E.E.C. scheme also embodied a particularly restrictive safeguard system based on product-by-product ceiling limitations. As might be expected, the G.S.P. ceilings were especially restrictive on products of export interest to the African Associates which could also be supplied in large volume by other beneficiaries, for example plywood, articles of wood and goat and kid leather.

The United Kingdom faced similar pressures from the Commonwealth developing countries and territories.* In considering their trading interests the U.K. G.S.P. scheme excluded most agricultural products and many industrial products of export interest to the Commonwealth developing countries. However, there still remained a large number of industrial products that were included in the U.K. G.S.P.; in this regard the United Kingdom was much more liberal towards the non-Commonwealth developing countries than the E.E.C. was towards the non-Associates. There is little doubt that Commonwealth developing-country exporters of these products suffered somewhat because of the U.K. G.S.P. The magnitude of this injury is difficult to quantify but, in any event, is now a moot point due to the United Kingdom's accession to the E.E.C.

The enlargement of the E.E.C. further complicated the already complex trading arrangements between developed European countries and the various groups of developing countries. In the first place, decisions had to be reached regarding the access to U.K. and Irish markets of African Associates' exports, the access to E.E.C. markets of Commonwealth developing countries' exports, and the access to Danish markets for both groups of developing countries. In essence completely new trading arrangements had to be negotiated. Second, the separate G.S.P. schemes of the United Kingdom, Ireland, Denmark and the E.E.C. had to be merged into one. And third, how were the trading interests of the other European nations to be considered as the United Kingdom, Ireland and Denmark pulled out of EFTA? Special arrangements were needed here as well. Thus the E.E.C. of nine was required to modify its international trading arrangements regarding associated developing countries, regarding G.S.P. treatment for other developing countries, and regarding its trading relations with the other countries of Western Europe. These arrangements will be discussed in turn.

---

* At that time the following developing countries enjoyed Commonwealth preferences in U.K. markets: Barbados, Botswana, Burma, Cyprus, Fiji, Gambia, Ghana, Guyana, India, Jamaica, Kenya, Lesotho, Malawi, Malaysia, Mauritius, Nigeria, Pakistan, Sierra Leone, Singapore, Sri Lanka, Swaziland, Tanzania, Trinidad and Tobago, Uganda, and Zambia.

MODIFICATIONS IN THE ASSOCIATION ARRANGEMENTS

At the time the E.E.C. was enlarged (1 January 1973) the Yaoundé Convention and the Arusha Agreement were in mid-term – they were scheduled to expire simultaneously by 31 January 1975 at the latest. During the enlargement negotiations, the status for Commonwealth countries was resolved by inviting a number of the developing Commonwealth countries to associate under a new convention which was to also cover the Yaoundé and Arusha countries. The countries which were not invited to associate were the developed and the Asian developing Commonwealth countries.* In addition, Gibraltar and Hong Kong did not receive special status even though the other U.K. territories were granted access to E.E.C. markets on a level with E.E.C. member-state territories. It was argued that the trading interests of these 'non-associable' countries and territories would be safeguarded by the G.S.P. provisions, guaranteeing these countries and territories duty-free access to E.E.C. markets for their industrial exports.

The negotiations with the 'associable' developing countries in Africa, the Caribbean and the Pacific (the so-called 'A.C.P. countries') began in Brussels in mid-1973 and culminated in the Lomé Convention (named after the concluding January–February 1975 meeting held in Lomé, Togo).†

The major provisions of this convention relevant to the G.S.P. are as follows:

(1) The principle of non-reciprocity governs E.E.C. concessions, i.e. the A.C.P. countries do not grant 'reverse' preferences in favour of imports from the E.E.C. This provision was included at the request of the A.C.P. countries so they could enjoy G.S.P. treatment under the U.S. scheme (see Chapter 3).

(2) All industrial products would be admitted to the E.E.C. duty-free without ceiling limits.

(3) Unlimited duty-free access will apply to those agricultural products for which customs duties (excluding variable levies) are the only form of protection against imports. For the other agricultural products the E.E.C. will normally grant A.C.P. states more favourable treatment than that accorded third-country suppliers. In addition, these other agricultural items would be considered, on an individual basis, for special arrangements. Three such agreements have already been signed, covering sugar, rum and ban-

---

* Thus Bangladesh, India, Malaysia, Pakistan, Singapore and Sri Lanka were excluded. In January 1972 Pakistan withdrew from the Commonwealth in protest against the forthcoming diplomatic recognition of Bangladesh by Australia, New Zealand and the United Kingdom.
† The forty-six A.C.P. countries are: in Africa the nineteen Yaoundé countries, including Mauritius, the three Arusha countries, Botswana, Gambia, Ghana, Lesotho, Malawi, Nigeria, Sierra Leone, Swaziland, Zambia, Ethiopia, Equatorial Guinea, Guinea, Guinea-Bissau, Liberia and Sudan; in the Caribbean Bahamas, Barbados, Grenada, Guyana, Jamaica, and Trinidad and Tobago; in the Pacific Fiji, Tonga and Western Samoa.

anas. Under the sugar agreement, for example, the E.E.C. has agreed to buy a minimum annual volume at guaranteed prices to be renegotiated annually.

(4) In order to facilitate industrial integration in Africa, the rules of origin governing A.C.P. trade will be administered on a full cumulative basis not limited by African regional groupings.

In addition the Lomé Convention provides for roughly $4·5 billion in aid to the A.C.P. countries, to be allocated over a four-year period. The aid consists of $2·75 billion in grants, $1·07 billion in loans, $0·1 billion in risk capital and $0·5 billion in funds (STABEX) to be used to stabilise the export earnings of A.C.P. countries' major products (a major product is defined as any product for which E.E.C. imports account for more than 7·5 per cent of a country's total export earnings).

It is obvious that the Lomé Convention provides the A.C.P. countries better access to E.E.C. markets than they would enjoy if they had to depend on the G.S.P. instead. The product coverage is broader, there are no value limits to preferential trade (except under the special agricultural-item agreements), the preferential duty cuts on agricultural products are larger, and cumulative origin is granted. Thus for all practical purposes the A.C.P. countries cannot be considered as 'real' beneficiaries under the E.E.C. G.S.P. even though they are 'formally' listed as beneficiaries.*

Just like the A.C.P. countries, all of the Mediterranean policy trade agreements had to be renegotiated after the E.E.C. enlargement. The 'formal' beneficiaries that are *de facto* non-beneficiaries in practice because of their more favourable treatment under an association agreement are Algeria, Cyprus, Egypt, Lebanon, Morocco and Tunisia.† In addition, the E.E.C. has agreements with Israel, Malta and Spain. Although these countries are not G.S.P. beneficiaries, their association with the E.E.C. does have implications for the G.S.P. benefits of other developing countries – exports from these Associates will now compete on a duty-free basis with exports from the G.S.P. beneficiaries.

CHANGES IN THE G.S.P. SCHEMES

In January 1974 the United Kingdom, Denmark and Ireland began participating in the joint E.E.C. scheme of generalised preferences. Consequently, their existing (more liberal) G.S.P. schemes disappeared. Although this is an *ex post* fact and does not really enter into the continuing evolution of E.E.C. trade policy relating to the developing countries, it is indicative of the degree to which the E.E.C. is willing to sacrifice the trade interests of developing

* The only developing countries that *really* benefit from the E.E.C. G.S.P. are the Asian and most Latin American developing countries and the developing territories of non-E.E.C. member states (but including Hong Kong and Gibraltar).
† Jordan and Syria will soon begin negotiating association agreements with the E.E.C.

countries in general for improvements in trade relations with selected developing-country 'friends'.

When the G.S.P. schemes of the United Kingdom, Denmark and Ireland were adapted to that of the E.E.C., two major changes were involved: (1) certain products which qualified for G.S.P. treatment under the individual schemes of the joiners were excluded from the new E.E.C. scheme; and (2) preferential trade which was unrestricted under the individual schemes of the joiners was brought under the ceiling limitations of the new E.E.C. scheme.

The most important change in the product coverage concerned industrial raw materials, which are excluded from the new E.E.C. G.S.P. Formally, such products entered the United Kingdom, Denmark and Ireland under duty-free M.F.N. or G.S.P. tariff treatment; but since the joiners must also adopt the E.E.C. common external tariff, these products became subject to duty – with definite adverse effects on the export interests of the G.S.P. beneficiaries. Although agricultural products were generally excluded from the joiners' schemes as well as from the scheme of the E.E.C. of six, the United Kingdom, Denmark and Ireland did treat agricultural products more liberally than the E.E.C.: (1) more products were included; and (2) the products qualified for much deeper G.S.P. tariff reductions. A final change in product coverage of lesser importance involves the textile sector. In general the joiners excluded all textiles from their G.S.P. schemes whereas the E.E.C. 'appeared' more liberal here by including all such products. However, the major textile items – cotton textiles covered by the Long Term Cottom Arrangement (L.T.A.) *and* substitute products – qualified for G.S.P. tariffs only if the exporting beneficiary country abided by the L.T.A. 'voluntary' export restrictions, thereby limiting their export expansion to the 5 per cent growth rate dictated under the L.T.A. Thus textile trade will not really benefit from the G.S.P.

The application of the ceiling limits to G.S.P. trade was thoroughly examined in the previous chapter – suffice it to say that 'effective' product coverage under the E.E.C. scheme is substantially below the level of E.E.C. imports of G.S.P. products from the G.S.P. beneficiaries because of the system of ceiling limitations.*

Finally, the implications of E.E.C. enlargement on the status of beneficiary developing countries depends on which countries enjoy special tariff treatment and which countries do not. It has already been argued that the A.C.P. countries are 'more preferred' – under the Lomé Convention rather than the G.S.P. The second echelon of preferred status is reserved for those developing countries coming under the E.E.C. Mediterranean policy. The 'real' G.S.P. beneficiaries come behind these groups as their duty-free treatment

---

* The G.S.P. industrial product coverage was reduced from $1,090 million to an 'effective' G.S.P. coverage of only $353 million (see Table 7.3).

on industrial products is subject to ceiling limits and their agricultural product coverage is chosen not to assist their export prospects (as is the case for
the A.C.P. and Mediterranean countries) but to protect E.E.C. producers
and the export prospects of the E.E.C.'s 'friends'. (This is some compensation
to the Asian Commonwealth countries which lost their unrestricted preferences in the U.K. market while being denied association opportunities.)
Next come the non-beneficiaries, which are contracting parties to GATT
and thereby enjoy M.F.N. tariff treatment, i.e. mainly other developed countries. Finally come the socialist countries of Eastern Europe which often face
tariffs which discriminate against their exports. Thus G.S.P. treatment gives
the 'real' G.S.P. beneficiaries preferred status over these last two groups of
countries only. But this too is subject to change.

AN ENLARGED EUROPEAN FREE-TRADE AREA

Prior to the E.E.C. enlargement Western Europe was divided into two major
trading blocks – the E.E.C. of six and the European Free Trade Area
(EFTA) consisting of the E.E.C. joiners (the United Kingdom, Denmark and
Ireland) and seven other countries (Finland, Norway, Sweden, Austria, Switzerland, Portugal and Iceland). The withdrawal of the United Kingdom,
Ireland and Denmark from EFTA was a serious blow to the significance of
intra-EFTA trade. As a result, the E.E.C. initiated a series of individual talks
with the non-acceding members of EFTA which resulted in free-trade
agreements with each of the seven. These free-trade agreements call for a
phasing in of unrestricted reciprocal duty-free treatment covering West European trade in manufactured products, including processed agricultural and
fishery items; by 1977 such trade will be fully duty-free.

The consequences of this new European free-trade area for manufactured
products for the G.S.P. beneficiaries can hardly be exaggerated. Under the
G.S.P. scheme of the E.E.C., the 'real' G.S.P. beneficiaries will no longer
enjoy preferential treatment over West European producers; in fact they are
less preferred: (1) because the G.S.P. contains ceiling limits which are absent
from the free-trade agreements; and (2) processed agricultural articles which
are generally excluded from the G.S.P. are contained in the free-trade
agreements. The 'real' G.S.P. beneficiary exports receive preferred status
only over exports from the United States, Japan, Australia, New Zealand,
South Africa, Rhodesia, China and the socialist countries of Eastern Europe.
In all likelihood developing-country exports do not compete heavily with
exports from these non-preferred countries.

And what about the G.S.P. trade benefits under the other West European
schemes? It is true that the developing countries are not divided into different hierarchies of preferred status; but they are second-class competitors in
comparison to E.E.C. producers who export to the other seven. Obviously,

the value of all European G.S.P. schemes has been seriously eroded by these agreements. The importance of this erosion is examined in the following section.

THE EROSION OF G.S.P. TRADE BENEFITS

To determine the negative impact of E.E.C. enlargement on G.S.P. trade one must first identify the original trade benefits accruing from the G.S.P. as introduced. This initial benefit consists of two elements:

(1) beneficiary exports displace domestic production, including intra-E.E.C. trade, as a result of the G.S.P. tariff reductions – this is normally called 'trade creation' and is essentially unaffected by the E.E.C. enlargement since the G.S.P. tariff reductions are maintained; and

(2) beneficiary exports displace E.E.C. imports from non-preferred sources due to the preferential nature of the G.S.P. tariff reductions – this is normally called 'trade diversion' and is adversely affected by the E.E.C. enlargement to the extent that 'third countries' are transferred from an initial 'non-preferred' status to a 'more preferred' status, i.e. some initially non-preferred countries now receive access to E.E.C. markets, which is more favourable than that provided under the G.S.P.

Of course, both of these elements are important in determining the G.S.P. trade benefits for developing countries. But it is the second element that is important in determining the adverse impact on G.S.P. trade which is caused by E.E.C. enlargement, subsequent trade agreements under the Mediterranean policy and the revised nature of E.E.C.–EFTA trading relations. This conclusion is crucial, as the concept of preferential treatment is generally believed to be the main source of G.S.P. trade benefit.

Yet it cannot be over-emphasised that preferential tariff treatment is of value only if there are 'non-preferred' imports competing with G.S.P. trade. If there are no suppliers whose exports face M.F.N. (or higher) tariff rates, what is the benefit of 'preferential' treatment? To push this idea to an extreme, if the world today was governed by tariff-free trade, there would be no opportunity for preferential tariff treatment. On the other hand, the greater the number of exporting sources which face M.F.N. (or higher) tariff rates, the greater the opportunity for G.S.P. tariffs to provide meaningful trade benefits for developing countries.

The E.E.C. enlargement and subsequent events is a middle-ground modification in trade relations. A number of previously M.F.N. trading partners have gained tariff-free access to E.E.C. markets as a result of joining the E.E.C.,* participating in a new free-trade area for manufactured

* The United Kingdom, Ireland and Denmark.

products,* and participating in preferential trade agreements covering products of export interest to the signatories (including all industrial products).† In addition, a group of 'formal' G.S.P. beneficiaries now enjoy access to E.E.C. markets, which is more favourable than G.S.P. status.‡ Thus this latter group of countries changed from 'equal' competitors to 'more favoured' competitors *vis-à-vis* the 'real' G.S.P. beneficiaries. On the other hand, the first three groups of European and Mediterranean countries changed from 'less favoured' to 'more favoured'.

In addition to changing the value of G.S.P. access to the original E.E.C. markets, G.S.P. access to other markets is similarly affected:

(1) G.S.P. access to the United Kingdom, Ireland and Denmark is now less competitive than exports from the original six members of the E.E.C., the A.C.P. countries,§ and the Mediterranean policy countries;¶

(2) G.S.P. access under other EFTA-member G.S.P. schemes – Finland, Norway, Sweden, Austria and Switzerland – is now less favourable than that enjoyed by the original six members of the E.E.C. (the United Kingdom, Ireland and Denmark simply retain their 'more favoured' status).

Given these changes in the trade relations of West European countries, what remains of the G.S.P.? This of course depends upon who the remaining M.F.N. (or higher) tariff-rate countries are. The G.S.P. will continue to provide developing countries with access to European markets, which is more favourable than that enjoyed by several non-European developed countries, mainly the United States, Japan, Canada, Australia, New Zealand and South Africa. The East European countries will also continue to be 'less preferred'.

Since the value of preferential treatment depends on the ability of G.S.P. exports to displace exports from other sources, *what remains* of the G.S.P. depends upon the extent to which the 'real' G.S.P. beneficiaries export products which are also exported by the United States, Japan, Canada, and so on, or East European countries. Similarly, the *loss* of G.S.P. trade benefits depends upon the extent to which G.S.P. beneficiaries' exports compete in E.E.C. markets with exports from the United Kingdom, Ireland, Denmark, other EFTA countries and the non-beneficiary Mediterranean countries (mainly Spain, Turkey, Greece and Malta), as well as the extent to which

---

* Finland, Norway, Sweden, Austria, Switzerland, Iceland and Portugal.

† The Mediterranean countries of Spain, Malta, Greece and Turkey.

‡ The A.C.P. countries and the Mediterranean countries of Algeria, Morocco, Tunisia, Egypt, Israel, Lebanon, Cyprus, and possibly in the near future Jordan and Syria.

§ The original Commonwealth developing countries had preferential access which fell short of duty-free access.

¶ The EFTA countries retain their original duty-free access to these countries and therefore retain their 'more favoured' status.

their exports compete with exports of the initial E.E.C. member states in EFTA markets (Finland, Norway, Sweden, Austria and Switzerland). In essence the G.S.P. trade benefits under all West European schemes are eroded to the extent that intra-West European trade competes with G.S.P. beneficiary exports; and the G.S.P. retains value to the extent that beneficiary exports compete in West European markets with imports from the non-European developed countries and East European countries.

The UNCTAD Secretariat has examined this question in an attempt to quantify the magnitude of this erosion element in the G.S.P. The approach compares E.E.C. imports from G.S.P. beneficiaries with E.E.C. imports from competing sources on a product-by-product basis.* In those cases where G.S.P. beneficiary exports compete with non-European developed-country exports or exports from Eastern Europe, the value of the G.S.P. remains; and where the source of competition is EFTA or Mediterranean countries, the value has been eroded. Aggregate data resulting from this examination are given in Table 8.1 to indicate the general order of magnitude of the erosion element as well as the value of what remains.† Over half of all industrial imports of the original E.E.C. represents intra-E.E.C. trade. Thus the scope for trade creation (beneficiary exports displacing 'domestic' production, defined to include intra-E.E.C. trade) is quite large. Of the remaining trade, 5 per cent is accounted for by 'formal' G.S.P. beneficiaries and 38 per cent by countries who were 'non-preferred' when the G.S.P. was first introduced in 1971.‡

The enlargement of the E.E.C. and the subsequent creation of the European free-trade area with other EFTA countries converts half of this 38 per cent 'non-preferred' trade into 'more preferred'. The Mediterranean policy adds up to another 3 per cent of E.E.C. imports to the 'more preferred' category. The remaining 'non-preferred' sources (i.e. the United States, Japan, Canada, and so on, and East Europe) account for 16 to 19 per cent. Thus in the aggregate roughly half of the initial scope for G.S.P. trade to displace 'non-preferred' trade has been eliminated.

A more detailed examination was also conducted by sub-dividing industrial trade into four product categories:

(1) *A minimum erosion category* – products for which the remaining 'non-preferred' sources are significant suppliers to the E.E.C. market *and*

* No actual examination of the erosion of G.S.P. benefits under the EFTA G.S.P. schemes was conducted. However, we can anticipate that the erosion elements in these schemes will be similar to that of the E.E.C. scheme.

† Agricultural products were excluded from the UNCTAD study because of the host of non-tariff barriers imposed against such trade.

‡ The UNCTAD study did not separate the A.C.P. country trade from 'real' G.S.P. beneficiary trade. To the extend that such trade competes, the UNCTAD study underestimates the extent of the erosion in the G.S.P.

TABLE 8.1

Distribution of E.E.C. imports, 1970
(percentage shares)

Exporter groups	All industrial products covered by G.S.P.	Product categories[1]			
		I	II	III	IV
Pre-E.E.C. enlargement					
E.E.C. imports from world	100	100	100	100	100
intra-E.E.C. trade	57	52	32	60	63
'Formal' G.S.P. beneficiaries[2]	5	6	6	1	13
Pre-E.E.C. enlargement ('non-preferred')[3]	38	42	62	39	24
Post-E.E.C. enlargement					
Pre-enlargement ('non-preferred')	38	42	62	39	24
Countries gaining 'preferred' status					
Joined E.E.C.[4]	8	8	16	8	6
Entered free-trade area[5]	11	12	12	12	8
Under Mediterranean policy[6]	0–3	0–6	0–4	0	0–8
Countries remaining 'non-preferred'					
Non-European developed[7]	16	16	30	19	2
Eastern Europe[6]	0–3	0–6	0–4	0	0–8
Share of pre-enlargement 'non-preferred' trade which remains 'non-preferred'					
min[6]	42	38	48	49	8
max[6]	50	52	55	49	42

1. The four product categories are defined on pp. 131–3.
2. Includes 'real' beneficiaries and the 'formal' though not effective beneficiaries, namely the A.C.P. countries and the Mediterranean beneficiaries of Morocco, Tunisia, Algeria, Egypt, Lebanon and Cyprus. Unfortunately the data do not distinguish between 'formal' and 'real' beneficiaries.
3. The E.E.C. joiners, other EFTA, non-European developed countries, Mediterranean non-beneficiaries and East European countries.
4. The United Kingdom, Ireland and Denmark.
5. Finland, Norway, Sweden, Austria, Switzerland, Iceland and Portugal.
6. The additional Mediterranean countries are Spain, Turkey, Greece, Israel and Malta. The data include trade for these Mediterranean countries and East European countries that should be sub-divided into 'preferred' and 'non-preferred'. Hence only crude minimum and maximum estimates could be generated.
7. The United States, Japan, Canada, Australia and New Zealand.
SOURCE: UNCTAD Secretariat, reported in document *TD/B/C.5/8*.

beneficiary exports are constant or growing. This category accounts for 20 per cent of developing-country exports to the E.E.C.

(2) *A minimum erosion category* – similar to (1) except that beneficiary exports are declining. This category accounts for a negligible share of developing-country exports to the E.E.C.

(3) *A potential G.S.P. category* – similar to (1) except that beneficiary exports account for a negligible share of the E.E.C. market. Some of

these products may be potential growth products and thus cannot be given appropriate weight in the quantitative estimates. This category accounts for 17 per cent of developing-country exports to the E.E.C.

(4) *A significant erosion category* – products for which the remaining 'non-preferred' countries account for a zero or insignificant share of the E.E.C. market. This category accounts for 63 per cent of beneficiary exports to the E.E.C.

In the first three categories the opportunity for G.S.P. trade to displace initial 'non-preferred' trade* has been roughly cut in half; however, the scope for displacing remaining 'non-preferred' trade is still significant relative to the existing level of beneficiary exports to the E.E.C. Thus the remaining value of the G.S.P. is significant. These categories account for just over one-third of G.S.P. trade. In the fourth category, which accounts for almost two-thirds of beneficiary trade, the picture is reversed; the scope for displacing 'non-preferred' trade has been cut from 60 to 90 per cent. Existing beneficiary exports to the E.E.C. significantly exceed the trade flow, which remains 'non-preferred'. To put it somewhat differently, almost two-thirds of beneficiary trade with the E.E.C. involves products which the E.E.C. does not import (or imports in minor volumes) from the remaining 'non-preferred' sources, mainly the United States, Japan, Canada, Australia, New Zealand, South Africa and Eastern Europe.†

This examination of the erosion effect of the E.E.C. enlargement and subsequent events is limited to the impact on G.S.P. access to the initial six E.E.C. markets; its impact on G.S.P. access to other West European markets was ignored.‡ But, obviously, as the other West European countries gain 'more preferred' access to E.E.C. markets, so do the six E.E.C. countries gain 'more preferred' access to their markets. Consequently, the value of these G.S.P. schemes will be eroded – to the extent that G.S.P. trade competes with E.E.C. exports to these West European countries.

Whereas the product-by-product breakdown of E.E.C.–EFTA trade is not readily available, a rough order of magnitude of this trade is indicated by

* Including the United Kingdom, Ireland, Denmark, other EFTA countries and non-beneficiary Mediterranean countries.

† The UNCTAD report states that the product categories were determined on the basis that remaining 'non-preferred' sources included only non-European developed countries. If East European sources were also included, two-thirds of category (4) products would be transferred to category (1). However, since Eastern European exports account for at most 8 per cent of E.E.C. imports of category (4) products (relative to a 13 per cent market share for beneficiaries), the transferred products would, by and large, provide only limited opportunity for G.S.P. trade to displace remaining 'non-preferred' trade. Moreover, since East European export prices are not market prices in the traditional sense, it is difficult to determine the extent to which G.S.P. tariff advantages would place East European exports at a competitive disadvantage.

‡ We are here ignoring the United Kingdom, Ireland and Denmark, who already enjoyed 'more preferred' access under their EFTA membership.

data contained in Table 8.1. For all industrial products those members of
EFTA which did not join the E.E.C. account for 11 per cent of total E.E.C.
imports (25 per cent if intra-E.E.C. trade is excluded). Over all, the intra-
West European trade accounts for over three-quarters of E.E.C. imports. If
this same order of magnitude applies in the other West European countries
as well, we can conclude that, in the main, West European countries tend to
trade amongst themselves rather than with non-Europeans.

In this case, what is the scope for the continued beneficial operation of the
G.S.P.? It appears unlikely that much of the G.S.P. exports to any of the
West European markets will involve products which are also imported from
non-European developed countries. This is even more dramatic when
the traditional export products of these two groups are compared.
The highly industrialised countries (i.e. the United States, Japan, Canada,
and so on) are unlikely to concentrate in the exportation of the standardised,
unsophisticated and labour-intensive products which are so common in
developing-country export patterns. It is much more likely that the non-
West European competitors of the G.S.P. beneficiaries are the Mediterranean countries and countries of Eastern Europe. The first group will enjoy:
(1) access to E.E.C. markets, which is more favourable than that accorded
under the G.S.P.; (2) equal access to Austrian and Swiss markets as a result
of their beneficiary status under the G.S.P.; and (3) less favourable access to
Finland, Norway and Sweden, where they face M.F.N. tariffs. The East
European countries are always 'less preferred' (though sometimes they
receive M.F.N. treatment). But what does this mean? Since prices are not
really market prices in the traditional sense, is it reasonable to think that
G.S.P. treatment would put East European exporters at a price disadvantage? Or would they simply adjust their prices downward to meet the
market? It is difficult to predict, although it is likely that significant export
displacement caused by G.S.P. treatment would lead to defensive price
adjustments to maintain their place in the market.

Finally, some definite qualifications must be inserted. In the first place, the
above analysis is based on a static comparison of pre-G.S.P. trade patterns.
No attempt was made to adjust the data so as to take into consideration the
changes in trade patterns that might be induced by the G.S.P. tariff margins.

Second, the erosion concept is not intended to indicate that beneficiary
exports would actually decline. Instead the implication is that G.S.P. exports
will grow slower as a result of the erosion. After all, the E.E.C. enlargement
and subsequent formation of the West European free-trade area is likely to
have dynamic growth effects for Western Europe. Such stimulation in economic growth is likely to generate an increase in imports from non-European
sources as well as an increase in intra-Europe trade. In fact past studies of
the effects of the formation of the E.E.C. and EFTA demonstrate that these
dynamic growth elements are much more important than the traditionally
measured static benefits. These dynamic elements might so stimulate im-

ports from the developing countries that the beneficiaries end up better off even after considering the erosion cost. But in this case the G.S.P. will be playing a less important role in the international trade policies of the developing countries. If this erosion of the importance of the G.S.P. is to be minimised, definite revisions in the rules governing the operation of the European G.S.P. schemes are in order.

First, the concept of duty-free G.S.P. treatment should enable the developing countries to gain access to European markets under terms that are not less favourable than those enjoyed by other exporters; that is to say, the G.S.P. provisions should be at least as liberal as the European free-trade-area provisions – the product coverage should be as broad (including processed and semi-processed agricultural products which are part of the free-trade area but not the G.S.P.) and the G.S.P. ceiling limits should be abolished.

In addition, the G.S.P. should be improved beyond the range of the free-trade area in order to compensate the developing countries for the loss of preferential advantages. After all, the improvements in the G.S.P. which were just suggested are necessary to prevent the G.S.P. beneficiaries from being *discriminated against*. Additional improvements could be made in the area of agricultural commodities, programmes to stabilise export earnings (as contained in the Lomé Convention), more liberal treatment for the textile trade, and so on.

Without these minimal improvements the G.S.P. schemes of the European donors will provide trade benefits to the developing countries that fall far short of that promised during the G.S.P. negotiations. Promises that are given in the spirit of international co-operation should be kept, not given with one hand and taken away with the other. If these European schemes are allowed to be eroded away by subsequent events, the G.S.P. that took seven years to negotiate and five more to implement will be reduced to the schemes of the United States, Japan, Canada, New Zealand and Australia and the 'preferential measures' offered by certain East European developed countries. These remaining donor countries are unlikely to continue to operate their schemes in the spirit in which they were introduced. Efforts to identify troublesome aspects of the schemes and to improve their operation will fall on deaf ears.

9

M.F.N. Tariff Reductions and the G.S.P.

Soon after the introduction of the first G.S.P. scheme in 1971 and before the United States introduced the last scheme in 1976, the big three G.S.P. donors (the United States, the E.E.C. and Japan) set the stage for a new round of multilateral tariff negotiations (the so-called M.T.N.). As of this date, the negotiations have not yielded any concrete results but are still actively proceeding. If the end-result is anything like that which emerged from the Kennedy Round, where duties on manufactured products were reduced by an average of 35 per cent, this new round of tariff negotiations will have dire implications for the continuing value of the G.S.P. as a trade policy benefiting the developing countries.

The developing countries have repeatedly expressed public concern that M.F.N. tariff reductions will reduce the G.S.P. tariff margins – many of which are already very low. They fear that the margins will fall so low as to be inconsequential to importers in their decisions concerning sources for import supplies.

In light of the M.T.N. and its potential erosion of the value of the G.S.P. preferential tariff margins, the developing countries feel that they must evolve a united strategy from which to participate in the GATT round of tariff negotiations. Such a strategy might emphasise preserving the benefits of the G.S.P.; or, alternatively, in light of the shortcomings of the G.S.P., the developing countries might gain more from better M.F.N. access to developed-country markets than they lose from the simultaneous erosion of the value of the G.S.P. This chapter examines such a trade-off.

STRATEGY TO PROTECT THE G.S.P.

At the preparatory meeting for this new round of negotiations, held in Tokyo in September 1973, it was agreed that special consideration be given to the trade interests of the developing countries. It was formally declared that: (1) the M.T.N. should not injure the trading opportunities which the developing countries already enjoyed (including the G.S.P.); and (2) the M.T.N. should provide new additional trading opportunities. Such a statement, of course, means different things to different countries. The developed countries intended this to mean that after the M.T.N.-negotiated trade liberalisations are implemented, the developing-country trade opportunities *over all* would be better than prior to the M.T.N.; it was recognised that for some particular products they may lose. The developing countries emphasise, despite the initial shortcomings, that the G.S.P. can become an important and effective instrument for their benefit. Consequently, they feel that their opportunities under the G.S.P. must be safeguarded; the M.T.N. should take this into account and provide new opportunities for products not covered by the G.S.P.

The impact of M.F.N. tariff cuts on the G.S.P. depends on a number of factors such as: (1) the magnitude of M.F.N. tariff cuts; (2) the products chosen for M.F.N. cuts relative to the products covered by the G.S.P. and exported by the developing countries; (3) the time dimension chosen for phasing-in the M.F.N. cuts; (4) the extent to which future negotiations will lead to meaningful improvements in the G.S.P.; and (5) the ability of the developing countries to develop an export capability for non-traditional products. These last items incorporate future considerations into the current policy question. Based on an analysis of these factors by the UNCTAD Secretariat a developing-country strategy has evolved – in the extreme it is as follows:

(1) no M.F.N. cuts should be made on products covered by the G.S.P.;
(2) deep M.F.N. cuts should be made on products which are not now or never will be covered by the G.S.P.;
(3) the G.S.P. should be improved by (i) expanding the product coverage, (ii) expanding the duty-free provision to cover all G.S.P. products, (iii) eliminate all ceiling-type limitations on G.S.P. trade, (iv) liberalise the rules of origin, and (v) simplify the administrative provisions; and
(4) non-tariff barriers to trade affecting developing-country exports should be liberalised.

This strategy sounds like, and is, little more than a 'wish list'. In fact, the actual strategy is substantially more pragmatic, including, for example, the possibility that G.S.P. products will face M.F.N. tariff cuts. In this case, the strategy is for *smaller* M.F.N. cuts or *longer* phasing-in periods; and these considerations should govern existing G.S.P. products of current export interest, existing G.S.P. products of future export interest and existing export-interest products which might be included in the G.S.P. at a future date. The basic strategy is therefore to maintain as much of the current and potential G.S.P. as possible. For non-G.S.P. products, current or future, deep M.F.N. cuts are recommended, as well as the advanced implementation of such cuts for developing countries, i.e. on a preferential basis.

The extent to which the M.T.N. can effectively protect the G.S.P. or incorporate the developing-country strategy will depend on the modalities chosen to negotiate M.F.N. tariff reductions. For example, during the Kennedy Round the governing principle was that duties should be cut 'across the board', i.e. the tariff rate on every product should be reduced by 50 per cent.

But of course there were exceptions to this 50 per cent 'linear' rule; some sectors were excluded, others were subject to smaller duty reductions, and so on. When all was said and done, the actual reduction in tariff rates averaged roughly 35 per cent. We must also expect numerous exceptions to apply to the modality which is adopted for the current negotiations. But, more importantly, is the developing-country strategy consistent with the M.T.N. modalities?

The G.S.P. strategy calls for basically product-by-product negotiations – zero or small cuts on G.S.P. products, large cuts on others. In contrast, the negotiations to date have concentrated on pseudo-automatic formulas which would be applied across the board, with exceptions for sectors such as agriculture and textiles. The U.S. position is a continuation of the Kennedy Round precedent of linear cuts leading to a substantial reduction in the average level of tariffs. The E.E.C., on the other hand, presses for so-called 'tariff harmonisation', i.e. a reduction in the disparity among the various national tariff rates applied to the same product. The E.E.C. position is primarily aimed at the U.S. tariff structure, which contains either very high or very low duties; in comparison the common external tariff of the E.E.C. countries is relatively uniform as a result of the averaging procedure used to establish the common tariff rates when the E.E.C. was founded. To achieve harmonisation the E.E.C. has suggested that each tariff be reduced by its own percentage, for example a 10 per cent duty would be reduced by 10 per cent to become 9 per cent, a 50 per cent duty would be reduced by 50 per cent to become 25 per cent, and so on. Alternatively, the E.E.C. has also offered the rule of a 50 per cent reduction to a common tariff floor of, say, 10 per cent; for example, a 20 per cent duty would be reduced half-way to 10 per cent, to become 15 per cent, a 50 per cent duty would be reduced half-way to 10 per cent, to become 30 per cent, and so on. The United States has opposed both of these harmonisation formulas on the following grounds:

(1) the reduction in the average level of duties would be quite modest; and
(2) the reduction in the average level of duties would be much higher for the United States than for the E.E.C., i.e. the reciprocity among the developed countries would be unbalanced.

A third modality which is being considered is a so-called 'integrated sectoral approach' under which tariff and non-tariff barriers would be negotiated simultaneously for a particular product sector such as agriculture, textiles, electronics, steel, and so on. The United States is concerned that progress on the agricultural front would be too slow and unsatisfactory compared with progress in other sectors. In fact, this approach was used to remove, for all practical purposes, textiles from the M.T.N.; textile trade is now governed by the renewed 'Arrangement Regarding International Trade in Textiles' which came into force on 1 January 1974.

The sectoral approach is the only one that is in anyway consistent with the developing-country strategy to save the G.S.P. Under either the 'linear' or 'harmonisation' modalities, the developing countries will have to resort to negotiating 'exceptions to the general rule' in order to safeguard the G.S.P. preferential tariff margins.

The UNCTAD Secretariat has analysed developing-country exports to the E.E.C., Japan and the United States on a product-by-product basis to determine the extent to which the M.T.N. may erode the G.S.P. This analysis permits the identification of 125 products with annual trade flows in excess of $5 million each and developing-country exports subject to M.F.N. duties in excess of 5 per cent; forty-eight of these products are covered by the G.S.P. schemes and seventy-seven are not.* The developing countries would argue that special consideration for these products of proven export interest to developing countries should not pose much of an obstacle to a successful M.T.N. Presumably this means that the forty-eight G.S.P. products should be placed on the 'exceptions' list and the other seventy-seven given a high priority for inclusion in the G.S.P.

However, upon closer examination it is revealed that for fifteen of the forty-eight major G.S.P. products, the developing countries are the major suppliers. In such a case, the opportunity for G.S.P.-stimulated trade diversion in favour of the developing countries is quite limited; thus deep M.F.N. cuts would have only minimal if any adverse impact on developing-country exports. These fifteen products are accounted for by Japan (seven products) and the United States (eight products).† The E.E.C. accounts for none; however, the total E.E.C. trade figures include intra-E.E.C., intra-Europe and other 'more preferred' trade. As a consequence, the G.S.P. 'real' beneficiaries may actually be the major non-preferred suppliers for some of the sixteen major G.S.P. products accounted for by the E.E.C. To summarise, the G.S.P. is worth protecting for roughly thirty-three of the forty-eight major G.S.P. products: fifteen products under the U.S. G.S.P., only two for Japan, and at most sixteen products for the E.E.C. Thus the necessary 'exceptions' list to protect the major current export interests of the developing countries is quite modest.

But what about the seventy-seven major products not covered by the

* These 125 products account for over three-quarters of E.E.C., Japanese and U.S. imports of such products from the developing countries. These donor-country product counts are sixteen, nine and twenty-three, respectively, for G.S.P. products, and fifty-six, five and sixteen, respectively, for non-covered items. It should be noted that certain products have been excluded from consideration due to non-tariff barriers, namely textiles, shoes and petroleum.

† The seven products for Japan account for 93 per cent of Japan's imports of major G.S.P. products from the developing countries; the eight products for the United States account for only 30 per cent of such trade.

G.S.P. The choice of benefiting the developing countries' export interests via M.F.N. or G.S.P. tariff cuts is important only when there exists substantial M.F.N. trade. If the G.S.P. beneficiaries are the major suppliers, then any tariff reduction will be of equal benefit whether it is preferential or M.F.N. For the seventy-seven products identified as major non-G.S.P. items, the developing countries are major suppliers of forty-three – twenty-six (of fifty-six) in E.E.C. markets, four (of five) in Japanese markets and thirteen (of sixteen) in U.S. markets.* For these forty-three products M.F.N. tariff cuts would be almost as beneficial for the developing countries as having these products included in the G.S.P. On the other hand, the trade interests of the developing countries would be served if the other thirty-four products could be included in the G.S.P.; however, these products account for a relatively small share of donor–beneficiary trade in major non-G.S.P. products.

The major conclusion of this product-by-product analysis is that there is some validity in the strategy to preserve the G.S.P. However, the developing countries should not pursue it blindly. In some cases, the erosion of G.S.P. tariff margins will not adversely affect the trade interests of the beneficiaries. And in some other cases, the developing countries should not hold out for including a particular product in the G.S.P.; their trade interests will be served equally well by deep M.F.N. cuts. It is only when the developing countries are minor suppliers that G.S.P. preferential treatment is important; non-preferred M.F.N. suppliers must exist before trade-diversion incentives can operate to stimulate beneficiary exports.

OFFSETTING BENEFITS FROM M.F.N. TARIFF REDUCTIONS[1]

As previously indicated, the impact of M.F.N. tariff reductions on the export prospects of developing countries has both positive and negative elements. There is little doubt that across-the-board M.F.N. tariff cuts will erode part of the trade-diversion element of the G.S.P. Donor-country importers will have smaller price incentives to purchase from beneficiary exporters, as the preferential tariff margins would be reduced by the same amount as any reduction in M.F.N. tariffs; but at the same time the developing countries would benefit from M.F.N. reductions on three counts.

First, many products covered by the G.S.P. are denied G.S.P. tariff treatment because of the restrictive ceiling-type safeguards or because of rigid processing or administrative requirements under the rules of origin. However, M.F.N. tariff reductions on these products would generate trade-creation incentives that are not limited by ceilings and do not face special origin requirements.

Second, many important products of export interest to developing coun-

* The trade in these forty-three major supplier products accounts for 66, 93 and 86 per cent, respectively, of E.E.C., Japanese and U.S. imports of the seventy-seven major non-G.S.P. products.

tries are currently excluded from the G.S.P. It is true that many of these same products would also be excluded from any M.F.N. negotiations, especially textiles, shoes and petroleum. Nevertheless, we can anticipate that the M.F.N. negotiation round would cover a broader range of products than is presently covered by the G.S.P.

Third, G.S.P. tariff treatment is not available to all developing countries on an equal basis. For example, Taiwan is excluded from the E.E.C. scheme; Hong Kong faces special restrictions under the G.S.P. schemes of the E.E.C. and Japan; the Mediterranean countries are excluded from the schemes of the E.E.C. and the United States; the OPEC countries and Cuba are

TABLE 9.1

Costs and benefits of a 50 per cent M.F.N. tariff reduction
(annual 1970 trade flows in millions of U.S. dollars)

Cost/benefit	United States	E.E.C.	Japan	Others*	Total
Cost due to erosion of preference margins	16·5	3·5	0·5	7·5	28·0
Benefit from absence of value limits	28·0	98·0	24·0	0·0	150·0
Benefit from broader product coverage	11·3	9·6	9·7	—	30·6
Benefit to non-beneficiary developing countries	125·0	13·0†	6·0	—	144·0

* Benefits from broader product coverage and benefits to non-beneficiaries could not be estimated for the other donors.
† Excludes Spain under the presumption that an E.E.C.–Spain trade agreement is signed. If no such agreement is signed this figure would be increased by approximately $60 million.
SOURCE: UNCTAD Secretariat calculations; see UNCTAD documents *TD/B/C.5/34*, addendum 1, *TD/B/C.5/38*, addendum 1 and *TD/B/C.5/22*.

excluded from G.S.P. treatment in the United States; and so on. In contrast, all countries which are signatories of GATT would enjoy the full benefits of M.F.N. tariff reductions.

Estimates of the cost and various benefits of the proposed tariff negotiations are presented in Table 9.1.* These estimates are calculated under the assumption that 50 per cent M.F.N. tariff cuts were negotiated across the board and introduced while the G.S.P. continues in effect under the currently existing provisions and limitations.

The loss of G.S.P. benefits due to the erosion of preferential tariff margins

* The methodology and data used in these calculations were discussed in Chapter 7, pp. 101–6.

represents the loss of the developing countries' competitive advantage over non-beneficiary-country exports to the donors, i.e. the trade-diversion component of the G.S.P.-stimulated trade expansion. Since the M.F.N. reduction would amount to only 50 per cent of the initial tariff rates (rather than the 100 per cent reduction under the G.S.P.), only one-half of the trade-diversion element would be lost. Thus the loss of the G.S.P. benefits would amount to $28 million measured in terms of 1970 annual trade flows; this loss would occur only after the M.F.N. tariff reductions were fully phased in. These calculations ignore the effect of normal market growth rates which would adversely affect the benefits of the G.S.P. as more and more products come up against the ceiling-type limits. Thus these calculations tend to overstate the relative cost to developing countries of eroding the preferential tariff margins.

In contrast to this $28 million loss in annual trade flows, the benefits to those developing countries which currently enjoy G.S.P. status would be $150 million from 50 per cent tariff cuts on products currently affected by the ceiling-type limits, plus an additional $31 million from M.F.N. cuts on products currently excluded from the G.S.P. other than textiles, shoes, petroleum and the products defined as 'import-sensitive' in the U.S. Trade Act of 1974 – certain electronics, steel items, glassware, watches, and so on. In total, the trade advantages gained by the G.S.P. beneficiaries from M.F.N. tariff reductions amount to $181 million or 6·5 times the loss of G.S.P. advantages due to the erosion of preferential tariff margins. In total the beneficiaries gain $153 million in 1970 annual trade flows.

Finally, the benefits of M.F.N. tariff reductions accruing to those developing countries which do not enjoy the fruits of the G.S.P. – or other special access to E.E.C. markets – amount to $144 million in 1970 annual trade flows. If Spain does not succeed in negotiating a preferential trade agreement with the E.E.C., the benefits of 50 per cent M.F.N. tariff cuts to non-beneficiary developing countries would be increased by an additional $60 million, bringing the total to over $200 million annually. This M.F.N. trade advantage to the few non-beneficiary developing countries is roughly equal to the net M.F.N. advantage for the G.S.P. beneficiaries combined. This result is not too surprising as the non-beneficiaries are generally those developing countries lying on the border between 'developed' and 'developing'.

On the basis of this static analysis, there is little doubt about the benefits of M.F.N. tariff reductions to developing countries. Certainly non-beneficiaries have a strong interest in M.F.N. tariff reductions. But more importantly, the beneficiary developing countries taken together stand to gain more from M.F.N. tariff reductions than they lose from the resulting erosion of the G.S.P. as it is currently operating.

However, any static comparison of the trade benefits of the G.S.P. with and without M.F.N. tariff reductions overlooks certain factors. Most importantly, it overlooks the possibility of improvements in the G.S.P. such as expanded product coverage or relaxations of the ceiling-type limits. These improvements affect the trade prospects of G.S.P. beneficiaries in two ways. First, the more liberal the G.S.P., the smaller are the additional benefits which the beneficiaries would realise from M.F.N. tariff cuts. Second, the more liberal the G.S.P., the greater are the losses due to the erosion of G.S.P. tariff margins. In the extreme, if the G.S.P. covered all products subject to M.F.N. negotiations, and if the ceiling-type limits were completely eliminated, M.F.N. tariff reductions would simply erode the trade-diversion element of the preferential tariff margins without any offsetting benefits to the G.S.P. beneficiaries. Of course, any modifications in the G.S.P. leave the trade advantages of the non-beneficiary developing countries unaffected; their interest in M.F.N. tariff reductions is similarly unaffected.

The evaluation of the *pros* and *cons* of M.F.N. negotiations in light of a potentially liberal G.S.P. will be conducted under three possible situations. First, consider a G.S.P. expanded to cover all products subject to M.F.N. negotiations, i.e. all but textiles, shoes, petroleum and those products designated as 'import-sensitive' under the U.S. Trade Act of 1974. In this case the trade benefits accruing to G.S.P. beneficiaries would increase by $60 million annually – the bulk of this is trade creation which would not be affected by subsequent M.F.N. tariff reductions. If tariffs were then reduced by 50 per cent on an M.F.N. basis, one-half of the trade-diversion element would be lost to the beneficiaries at an annual cost of only some $2·5 million. The offsetting trade advantage to G.S.P. beneficiaries of M.F.N. cuts on products affected by the ceiling-type limits would be in the neighbourhood of $120 million annually. Thus the G.S.P. beneficiaries have more to gain from M.F.N. cuts than they lose even if the G.S.P. were to be expanded to cover the widest possible range of products. This conclusion again emphasises the seriousness of the ceiling-type limitations embodied in the G.S.P.

The second evaluation, therefore, considers a G.S.P. which does not contain any ceiling-type limits but is limited to the existing product coverage. The G.S.P. trade-expansion benefits for the beneficiary developing countries would almost double from just under $400 million to over $700 million – but again the bulk of this is accounted for by trade creation, which is not affected by subsequent M.F.N. tariff cuts. M.F.N. tariff reductions would reduce the trade-diversion element by only $41·5 million annually. However, the potential offsetting benefit is now limited to trade advantages coming from M.F.N. negotiations covering a wider range of products than the G.S.P. We have already seen that such opportunities are quite limited – the offsetting benefits would be less than $30 million for the G.S.P. beneficiaries. In this case the G.S.P. beneficiaries incur a net loss of slightly more than $10 million annually from M.F.N. tariff cuts, coming on top of a G.S.P. which has been liberalised by the elimination of all ceiling-type limitations.

Finally, if the G.S.P. were to be liberalised to cover the widest range of products, and if the ceiling-type limitations were to be eliminated, the beneficiaries would not gain any offsetting benefits from M.F.N. tariff reductions. They would only incur trade-diversion losses amounting to roughly $45 million annually. But this amounts to less than 2 per cent of the total $3·6 billion in 1970 beneficiary trade covered by the G.S.P.

What does all this imply for a united developing-country strategy regarding GATT tariff negotiations? First and foremost, an unequivocal opposition to M.F.N. tariff reductions is in the best interests of the G.S.P. beneficiaries *only if* the ceiling-type limitations are eliminated from the G.S.P.; and even in this case the annual trade advantages of protecting the G.S.P. by prohibiting M.F.N. tariff cuts are only in the range of $40 million. This relatively insignificant trade benefit to the G.S.P. beneficiaries as a group comes at the expense of roughly $200 million in forgone annual trade-flow benefits to non-beneficiary developing countries. But if the ceiling-type limits cannot be fully eliminated, or if the trade interests of non-beneficiary developing countries are also taken into consideration in a united GATT negotiation strategy, the benefit/cost balance swings very decidedly in favour of deep M.F.N. tariff cuts.

In the final analysis, then, the optimal developing-country strategy depends upon the future. How likely is it that the G.S.P. will be significantly improved? To date the improvements which have been negotiated are more cosmetic than real; and the improvements that have been made were introduced in conjunction with additional restrictions aimed primarily at the more advanced developing countries. This shows a concern on the part of the donors that domestic import-competing industries might be adversely affected by developing-country exports, especially when G.S.P. tariff treatment is enjoyed by such a large and diverse group of countries. So long as the more advanced developing countries enjoy the same G.S.P. access to donor markets as the other developing countries, the G.S.P. provisions are certain to contain a number of restrictions designed to safeguard firms and workers in the donor nations. Only if discrimination among the developing countries is introduced explicitly into the G.S.P., is it likely that significant improvements will be made. And with this discrimination a larger group of developing countries would be dependent upon GATT negotiations for improved access to world markets.

This introduces the primary element for evaluating the prospects of M.F.N. tariff reductions, namely: Which developing countries are of most concern? If one is primarily concerned with the poorer developing countries, the G.S.P. is an attractive commercial policy instrument. Generally these countries are not affected by the ceiling-type limitations on G.S.P. trade; nor should the developed countries be adverse to including in their schemes all products of export interest to them – provided the more advanced developing countries do not enjoy the same benefits. Under the current situation over three-quarters of G.S.P. trade can be accounted for by the following developing countries: Taiwan, Hong Kong, Mexico, Yugoslavia, South Korea, Brazil, Singapore, India, Peru, Chile, Argentina and Iran. These same countries account for over 95 per cent of the trade denied G.S.P. tariff treatment due to the ceiling-type limitations. For the remaining beneficiary developing countries, the G.S.P. is an open-ended system; M.F.N. tariff cuts would erode their G.S.P. trade advantages – small though they may be – with only very minor offsetting benefits.

On the other hand, if one is concerned about all developing countries, and in particular those most able to benefit from a trade (as contrasted with an aid) policy, then concern for the more advanced developing countries cannot be sacrificed in favour of the poorer. The G.S.P. schemes to date provide a limited benefit to many of these more advanced countries and no benefit to others. Generally speaking these countries would benefit more from a successful round of M.F.N. tariff reductions than from maintaining the existing G.S.P. tariff margins.

A final consideration for the developing countries may be a desire to keep the G.S.P. alive, with improvements being negotiated in the UNCTAD forum, which has proven to be sympathetic to the trade problems of developing countries. In contrast M.F.N. negotiations would come under the auspices of GATT, a forum which has generally de-emphasised the objective of economic development and has instead concentrated on reconciling the trade problems of the industrial nations. But with UNCTAD playing an advisory role to the developing countries as they approach the GATT negotiations, we should expect the trading interests of the developing countries to become a major item on the GATT agenda. It may be that the developed countries can be convinced that they should compensate the G.S.P. beneficiaries for the erosion of their preferential tariff margins. Such compensation could take the form of improvements in the G.S.P. schemes (though with smaller preferential margins), such as the elimination of ceiling-type limits and expanded product coverage, especially in the area of processed agricultural and fishery products. In this way the beneficiaries gain through compensation and the non-beneficiaries gain through M.F.N. tariff reductions. In this regard the beneficiaries could also negotiate an advanced implementation of M.F.N. tariff reductions on a preferential basis which would benefit them during the five years or so required to phase-in M.F.N. tariff reductions.

Thus the developing countries have an interest in maintaining an active presence in the GATT negotiations as well as pushing for conclusive agreements. In fact the developing countries stand more to gain or lose from GATT agreements regarding issues other than tariff rates, preferential or otherwise. After all, the existing M.F.N. tariff rates on manufactured products average only 10 percentage points. A major concern of GATT is non-tariff barriers to trade, many of which pose a more damaging barrier to developing-country exports than tariff rates, for example the programme of 'voluntary export restraints' to trade in textiles. A second concern of GATT is a potential revision of the escape-clause procedure. Given the recent history of such safeguard measures, it is important that the developing countries present a strong force against a new safeguard mechanism which is too liberal, a safeguard mechanism which could completely reverse the post-war tide towards freer access to world markets.

10
The G.S.P. and the 'New International Economic Order'

The developing countries first began the call for a new international economic order during the late 1950s. Their initial complaints stemmed from an impotence of domestic policy initiatives to speed their rates of economic development. They found themselves excessively dependent upon the developed community for the requisites of economic development – industrial machinery and technical expertise – requisites which they could not purchase in sufficient quantities due to inadequate foreign-exchange earnings (foreign aid was insufficient to fill the gap).

During the early post-war period developing-country exports were heavily concentrated in agricultural commodities and industrial raw materials. Such products faced unstable markets with wide price fluctuations, this led to export earnings which were subject to wide variations from year to year. It was felt that this problem could only be solved by export diversification, especially in the direction of manufactured products. In order to redress their disadvantaged position in the world economy, the developing countries called first for preferential access to developed-country markets for manufactured and semi-manufactured products. They argued that such treatment was necessary if developing-country exporters were ever to become competitive in world markets.

At the time, developing-country exporters of manufactured products faced two major problems. First, due to the limited scope of domestic markets, developing-country producers were constrained to sub-optimal scales of operation which naturally led to high production costs. These high processing costs existed even though wage rates were miserably low; in many cases the low wage rates were more than offset by even lower labour productivity leading to labour costs which were higher than those prevailing in the developed countries. In addition, developing-country exporters had to contend with higher cost and less frequent transport services, higher cost and less effective marketing and distribution channels, and so on. Furthermore, efficient manufacturing, which is heavily dependent upon readily accessible and low-cost material and component inputs, was made even more difficult by the import-substitution policies of many developing countries.

Second, the existing GATT-negotiated economic order, based on the principle of reciprocity, ignored the export interests of the developing countries. The resulting developed-country tariff profiles provided zero or low duties on raw materials and higher duties on products of higher-order processing.

Such escalated tariff structures encouraged the exportation of materials in their raw form rather than in the form of processed semi-manufactured or manufactured products. In essence these tariff structures granted very substantial protection to processing activities located in the developed countries.

To summarise, developing-country producers of manufactures simply could not compete on an equal basis with the sophisticated production and marketing firms of the industrialised world. Since developing-country exporters were 'less than equal' in the world economy, the developing countries argued, they should not be expected to compete on an equal (most-favoured-nation) basis; thus the call for 'more than equal' (preferential) treatment, i.e. the G.S.P.

WHAT IS THE VALUE OF THE G.S.P.?

The G.S.P. was never considered as a panacea for solving all the complex problems of development, but it was offered by the developed countries as an important new step to help the developing countries help themselves. It was envisaged that the price incentives created by the G.S.P. would lead to an increase in developing-country exports and export earnings, thereby contributing to industrialisation and economic development. While it is somewhat early to concretely evaluate the G.S.P., the evidence gained to date strongly indicates that the G.S.P. is not producing the expected results. The reasons for such a pessimistic conclusion derive from a number of sources.

(1) The pre-G.S.P. structure of developing-country trade was heavily concentrated on the exportation of zero-duty agricultural commodities and industrial raw materials. In fact such products accounted for 58 per cent of developing-country exports to the preference-giving countries of the West.

(2) When the G.S.P. was negotiated, the preference-giving countries decreed that the products to be covered by the system would, with few exceptions, be limited to manufactured industrial products and not processed and semi-processed agricultural products. Thus the scope of the G.S.P. was further reduced by 14 per cent of developing-country exports.

(3) Because of the protectionist political pressure of domestic import-competing producers, the preference-giving countries also excluded a number of industrial products of export interest to developing countries, reducing the product coverage of the G.S.P. by an additional 17 per cent (8 per cent excluding petroleum). The major exclusions are textiles and apparel (2 per cent) and electronic products deleted by the United States (2 per cent). Thus only 12 per cent of developing-country exports fall within the existing scope of the G.S.P.

But even this figure does not tell us what the value of the G.S.P. is to developing countries. Benefit is not measured by the existing trade which falls under the system, but instead by the effect which the preferential tariff margins have on expanding such trade. An important element in this regard is the special safeguard measures introduced by the preference-giving countries to protect their import-competing producers from unanticipated import injury. As seen in Chapter 5, the most restrictive elements are contained in the ceiling systems of the E.E.C. and Japan and the 'competitive-need' criteria of the United States. The U.S. provisions preclude G.S.P. tariff treatment for numerous products imported from particular 'competitive' developing countries, thereby denying G.S.P. treatment on 65 per cent of U.S. imports of G.S.P. products. The E.E.C. and Japan impose tariff quotas whereby preferential treatment would cease for the remainder of the year whenever a predetermined volume of G.S.P. trade was exceeded; G.S.P. tariff treatment would be reinstated at the beginning of the next year. While such re-opening of ceilings each year is more liberal than the U.S. provisions in terms of the volume of trade which actually receives G.S.P. tariff treatment, these tariff quotas are nevertheless equally restrictive in eliminating the tariff incentives for *expanded levels of trade*. These tariff quotas eliminate the trade-expansion benefits offered by the E.E.C. and Japanese schemes on 51 per cent and 86 per cent, respectively, of the trade that would otherwise receive G.S.P. treatment. These safeguard measures reduce the so-called 'effective' product coverage of the G.S.P. to only 7 per cent of developing-country exports to the donor countries.

The G.S.P. trade benefits, measured in terms of increased trade volumes, have been estimated to be in the neighbourhood of $500 million annually under rather liberal assumptions concerning the developing countries' ability to supply increased volumes of exports. It was also assumed that non-tariff barriers to beneficiary exports were non-operative and that the developing countries had no problem meeting the minimum processing requirements under the rules of origin. In reality such assumptions lead to estimates that overstate the benefits. For example, the best approximation is that one-quarter to one-third of the effective G.S.P. trade in manufactured products will be denied G.S.P. treatment because of a failure to meet rules of origin criteria. Thus we arrive at an annual G.S.P. trade-benefit estimate in the order of $350 million.

To interpret this $350 million as benefit to developing countries further assumes that all of the resources used to produce this expanded volume of trade were previously unemployed or redundant, thereby having zero opportunity costs. Obviously, this is not the case so the estimate must be further revised in a downward direction; but without even making this last adjustment, the G.S.P. benefits represent only 1 per cent of total developing-country exports to the preference-giving countries.

Even using the most charitable evaluation criteria leads to a conclusion that the G.S.P., as it operates today, is insignificant as a new trade policy to benefit the more than 150 developing countries designated as G.S.P. beneficiaries. Moreover, as shown in Chapter 7 (Table 7.4), over 80 per cent

of the effective G.S.P. trade is accounted for by only nine developing countries; the estimated benefits range up to roughly $50 million annually for
Taiwan, Mexico, Yugoslavia, South Korea and Brazil. And for the vast
majority of the beneficiary developing countries, the annual trade benefits
will average less than $0·5 million each, a very small amount for a new
international trade policy designed to help the developing countries help
themselves through trade rather than aid.

PROSPECTS FOR AN IMPROVED G.S.P.

It is hard to explain why such a tremendous effort was expended in negotiating and implementing a new system that would generate such meagre
benefits. If the limited benefits are the result of existing developing-country
trade patterns which may be expected to change drastically as a result of the
G.S.P., one might conclude that the G.S.P. has promise of some day generat-
ing meaningful trade benefits. In many respects the data support such an
hypothesis – almost three-quarters of developing-country exports to the
preference-giving countries enter duty-free or involve agricultural products,
and an additional 9 per cent is accounted for by petroleum. There is not
much scope for a tariff policy creating incentives for manufactured exports
to stimulate trade in duty-free, agricultural or petroleum products.

On the other hand, the hypothesis is somewhat refuted by examining the
remaining trade, which accounts for one-fifth of developing-country exports
to the G.S.P. donors. Almost half of this trade is excluded from the G.S.P.
outright, including such products as textiles and apparel, leather goods,
electronic items and miscellaneous other products. And over one-half the
remaining trade is 'sterilised' by the ceiling-type safeguard measures or by
restrictive minimum-processing criteria under the rules of origin. Thus
roughly three-quarters of the dutiable trade in industrial products does not
benefit from the G.S.P. because of limitations and restrictions imposed on
G.S.P. trade by the donor countries.

But does the risk of potential import-displacement injury to domestic
producers and workers justify such restrictive safeguard measures? After all,
if preferential tariff treatment is really an effective policy measure,
beneficiary exports of non-traditional products will increase substantially;
and this increased trade cannot help but adversely affect the production of
G.S.P. products in the donor countries. However, the estimates presented in
Chapter 7 (Table 7.6) place this potential problem in perspective; the G.S.P.,
even liberalised by eliminating the safeguard measures, would have an inconsequential impact on domestic production (displacing a very small frac-
tion of 1 per cent of output) and employment (displacing 50,000 workers).
The seriousness of this employment impact is minimal at most; the normal
annual change in manufacturing employment in the donor countries is
roughly 1·4 million jobs, or twenty-eight times larger than the G.S.P.-related

employment impact. Thus, in the aggregate, the G.S.P. would pose very minor employment-re-absorption problems.

This aggregate conclusion, however, should not be generalised to each manufacturing industry or to each regional or skill-class labour market. In fact we must suspect that certain industries and worker groups would be seriously affected by the G.S.P. It is concern for these cases that was paramount in the minds of donor-country policy-makers when the G.S.P. was introduced. The aggregate figures, however, indicate that this concern was excessive and resulted in G.S.P. regulations which were much more restrictive than necessary.

In such a circumstance one might suspect that as time and experience reveal the true costs of the G.S.P., meaningful improvements would be introduced. Unfortunately the experience to date has revealed an opposite tendency. While it is true that improvements have been introduced, the modifications in the G.S.P. regulations are more cosmetic than real; and the improvements which were made were introduced in conjunction with a number of additional restrictions. Over all the revisions in the regulations governing G.S.P. trade balance out against the developing countries as a group; a trend that can be expected to continue. After all the most influential pressures for revising the G.S.P. come from within the donor countries rather than from UNCTAD negotiations. When a particular industry lobbies for more restrictive treatment for a particular product because of increased import competition, it is more likely to be listened to than the rhetoric of generalities sermonised by developing countries in UNCTAD debates.

So how likely is it that the G.S.P. will be meaningfully improved in the future? The early indications are that the donors are extremely concerned about the export potential of the more advanced developing countries. To illustrate, the E.E.C. has introduced a number of new tariff quotas which only apply to pre-selected developing countries. So long as the more competitive beneficiaries enjoy the same access to donor markets as other developing countries, the G.S.P. is certain to contain a number of safeguard restrictions. Meaningful improvements will only come if discrimination among the developing countries is explicitly introduced. And this trend is beginning. Thus the G.S.P. seems to have a self-destruct mechanism with improvements being introduced in conjunction with additional restrictions imposed on those developing countries most capable of exporting manufactures. The G.S.P. potential is increased only for the truly non-competitive developing countries with the actual trade benefit remaining insignificant at best.

This self-destruct tendency is augmented by the events covered in Chapters 8 and 9; namely, the modifications in the rules governing trade among the countries of Western Europe and the on-going GATT negotiations to reduce M.F.N. tariffs. The events in Europe are leading to a West European free-trade area that will be fully operative sometime in 1977. Thus G.S.P. exports to Europe cannot receive access which is preferable to that enjoyed by all West European suppliers. The G.S.P. preferential tariff margins will apply only against West European imports from the non-European O.E.C.D. countries and the socialist countries of Eastern Europe. Put somewhat differently, the value of the G.S.P. will be eroded to the extent that G.S.P. exports compete with intra-West European trade; and this applies to all European G.S.P. schemes.

While it is somewhat early to predict the outcome of the GATT negotiations, it is probable that some reduction in M.F.N. tariff rates will occur. Obviously any M.F.N. tariff reduction will erode the value of the preferential tariff margins enjoyed by the G.S.P. beneficiaries.

Thus we arrive at a very dismal conclusion regarding the value of the G.S.P. to developing countries. First, the G.S.P. of today will generate quite modest trade benefits because many major products of export interest to developing countries have been excluded, and other important products come under excessively restrictive ceiling-type limitations or origin requirements. Second, the prospects for meaningful improvements in the G.S.P. provisions are quite dim because of the fear of import-displacement resulting from export expansion by the more advanced developing countries. Finally, the value of the G.S.P. is simultaneously being eroded by other events such as the West European free-trade area and the on-going GATT trade negotiations. But before concluding that developing-country export prospects in the manufacturing sectors are dim indeed, one should first ponder the question: Do developing countries really need preferential access to world markets? The answer to this question is, in many respects, no.

ALTERNATIVES TO STIMULATE MANUFACTURED EXPORTS

Obviously the developing countries enjoy an international comparative advantage for many manufactured products, such as textiles, leather goods, various electronics, toys and sporting goods. Undoubtedly numerous other products will be identified in the future. For any product in which the developing countries have a comparative advantage, preferential treatment *per se* is unnecessary. Freer access to world markets on an M.F.N. basis will enable them to expand sales at the expense of relatively less efficient domestic suppliers and to the benefit of importing-country consumers. The opportunities for preferential-tariff-induced trade diversion are minor in comparison, since the developing countries are already major exporters of these types of products. Note also that the high effective protection caused by escalated tariff structures can be redressed by *either* preferential or M.F.N. tariff reductions.

It might be argued that preferential tariff reductions are necessary because *all* developing countries do not have a comparative advantage for any particular product. Thus the preferential treatment is necessary to help the least competitive make inroads into markets previously served by non-beneficiaries. In reality, however, such opportunities will instead be exploited by those beneficiaries which have the international comparative advantage. The least competitive will still fail – unless the more competitive developing countries are discriminated against.

There is considerable evidence that the developing countries are capable of benefiting substantially from M.F.N. tariff cuts. For example, it has been shown that developing-country exports responded quite well to previous GATT-negotiated tariff reductions.[1] Also, the growth in developing-country trade under a little publicised provision in the U.S. tariff law has been phenomenal.* This so-called off-shore assembly provision (U.S. tariff items 806.30 and 807.00) permits the duty-free re-importation of components sent abroad for assembly; only that portion of the value of the final good which has been 'added' abroad is subject to duty. Even though this provision is available on an M.F.N. basis to any potential processing exporter, the developing-country trade coming under this 'off-shore' provision has grown more than three times faster than that of the developed countries; the annual growth rates are 60 and 18 per cent, respectively.[2] Obviously the developing countries can take advantage of improved access to world markets even when they must compete with industrial-country producers on an M.F.N. basis. This evidence demonstrates that the developing countries do have an international comparative advantage for certain products as well as for certain processing operations. They should take whatever steps they can to further reduce the tariff barriers facing their exports in these areas – even if the barriers are to be reduced on an M.F.N. basis. As the calculations in Chapter 9 show, the beneficiary developing countries have more to gain from M.F.N. tariff cuts than they stand to lose from the simultaneous erosion of their existing preferential tariff margins.

A final thought on M.F.N. tariff concessions concerns the product areas where tariff escalation causes the greatest harm, namely the initial stages of processing locally available raw materials. Normally, processing at this stage adds very little to the export value of the materials; consequently, even slight tariff escalation leads to substantial effective protection. If the developing countries could negotiate a reduction in duties on 'simply processed' agricultural commodities and industrial raw materials, such that the final duties on these 'simply processed' materials were not higher than the duties charged on the respective materials 'in raw form', the tariff discouragement against developing-country processing would be eliminated. Such a concession would often involve a very small tariff reduction for the developed countries.

But it should be recognised that such a policy would not necessarily solve

---

* Canada, Japan and most Western European countries also have similar provisions for reduced duty re-importation of components assembled off-shore.

the export problems of developing countries. Transport problems and costs are often much greater for products in a semi-manufactured form than in a raw form. For example, many processed agricultural products require special packaging and temperature control to preserve quality or taste. Alternatively, the raw-form product can often be shipped quite cheaply in open bulk for processing at the destination site. Other problems may occur which derive from different end-user quality-control requirements or consumer preferences. For example, consumers of ground coffee in one nation may demand a very different blend of coffee beans than consumers in a neighbouring country, or the purity of copper ingots required by one developed-country manufacturer may differ substantially from the purity requirements of another.

Such problems of consumer preferences or required manufacturer quality standards are unavoidable. But the elimination of the tariff escalation would place the developing-country processor on a level with the importing country's domestic processor, i.e. the tariff-induced discouragement to developing-country processing would be removed.

Another area in which improved access to world markets on an M.F.N. basis would significantly benefit the developing countries concerns non-tariff barriers to trade. The classic example here is the GATT 'Arrangement Regarding International Trade in Textiles' (the so-called new L.T.A. which covers natural and man-made fibre textiles and apparel), which provides for 'voluntary' export restrictions. This programme limits the growth in exports on products which the developing countries have a demonstrated comparative advantage. In this area the developing countries need no preferences, just open access to markets. Likely candidates for future 'orderly marketing arrangements' might include footwear, electronics, plywood and veneer, steel, toys and sporting goods, and many others. The developing countries would serve themselves quite well if they could simply stem this tide for increased protectionism, let alone obtain new concessions – preferential or otherwise. When these kinds of arrangements are imposed, a major determinant of a particular country's share of the 'allocated import market' is its historical market share. Thus the developing countries, individually and as a group, would receive a relatively small allocation for emerging products of export interest – products in which the international comparative advantage is in the process of shifting from developed to developing countries.

After all is said and done, there are numerous opportunities for developing countries to improve their prospects for exporting manufactured products through initiatives on a most-favoured-nation basis; but before leaving this issue it must be pointed out that one major deterrent to exporting manufactures is imposed by the developing countries themselves. Manufacturing is an activity which is heavily dependent on material inputs. On the average, roughly one-half of the cost of producing a manufactured product is accounted for by material inputs which are not produced in the manufacturing plant itself. Such inputs are normally purchased from another domestic firm, or they are imported.

During the early post-war period many developing countries embarked upon an inward-looking policy of import substitution by imposing high tariff walls to stimulate the domestic production of products which were then being imported. In the early stages these policies were quite effective in stimulating the production of non-durable consumer goods, thereby saving badly needed foreign exchange. Over time the import-substitution measures were modified towards 'increasing local content' of domestically sold products. The revised policy had important implications for many manufactured products which were initially produced for sale in the domestic market, primarily through the assembly of imported parts and components. The high tariff walls stimulated the local production of the most elementary parts and components; over time more of the inputs were being produced locally. However, because of limited scales of operation and other inefficiencies, these inputs were produced at costs much above comparable world prices; and consequently the finished manufactured products carry prices much above the world prices of competitive products. These products are competitive in local markets because of tariff protection, but they are not competitive in world markets. It has been estimated that this input-cost bias against exporting exceeds 100 per cent in most manufacturing industries located in several developing countries.[3] This means that the manufacturing process in the developing country must be twice as efficient as its counterpart in the developed countries before exporting is viable; and this ignores transport and importing costs which must be borne by the developing-country exporters but not by the developed-country import-competing producers.

If the developing countries are serious about export expansion in the manufacturing sectors, something must be done to improve the access of their manufacturers to crucial inputs. The most immediate way of treating this problem would be to directly subsidise exports to offset this input price disadvantage. Eliminating tariffs on material inputs is probably not politically feasible in the short run because of the import-displacement injury which would be incurred by the existing intermediate-goods producers. Similarly, a duty kick-back scheme for material inputs embodied in manufactured exports would also impinge on the traditional markets of the existing local producers of intermediate goods. Furthermore, the kick-back regimes would probably not be fully effective anyway; some manufacturers would remain dependent on locally produced high-cost inputs because of historical ties, vertical integration, or other such reasons. Over the longer run the governments would be well advised to gradually dismantle high protection for intermediate goods. This would improve the export prospects of domestic manufacturers of finished goods; it would also improve local efficiency by imposing competitive pressures on domestic producers of input goods. Some would fail, but those that remain would become competitive at world price levels.

This section has argued that the developing countries have attractive alternatives to the disappointing G.S.P. Some require negotiating initiatives in GATT, dealing with tariff and non-tariff barriers on an M.F.N. basis. Another was purely within the purview of each developing country. However, the major emphasis of the developing countries is in neither of these directions. Instead their heads and attention are turned in the direction of the United Nations, where delegates moralistically ponder what has come to be called the 'new international economic order'.

ELEMENTS OF THE 'NEW INTERNATIONAL ECONOMIC ORDER'

The negotiations for a 'new international economic order' cover two broad spectrums of concern to developing countries – international monetary matters and trade-related issues. The monetary matters are primarily those of increased financial aid and restructuring (reducing and/or canceling) the debt burdens of many developing countries. These would include the 'oil facility', reform of the International Monetary Fund, including the so-called 'link' between development assistance and S.D.R. creation, the 'gold sales', developing-country access to private capital markets, and so on. Since this book is concerned with trade matters the monetary elements of the 'new international economic order' will be bypassed.

The major trade-related elements of concern to the developing countries are improved access to developed-country markets for manufactured products (the subject of this book, i.e. the G.S.P.) and changes in the international marketing and pricing of primary commodities. These issues are of central importance to the so-called North–South debate taking place in the United Nations and at the periodic Paris meetings.

But there is a third item which has been de-emphasised during the North–South debate – and justifiably so because it is a policy which the developing countries have the power to introduce on their own. It is an area where the possibilities of economic progress have been demonstrated by example to be major – although the opportunities for political discord are similarly major, the reference is to economic integration among all or groups of developing countries.

Integration among developing countries

One major reason why developing countries have been unable to stimulate their own rates of economic growth through purely domestic policies is a simple technological constraint. Producing acceptable manufactured products of quality requires quite sophisticated and very expensive equipment and machinery. Man and machine then process material inputs into finished goods. Since the machinery costs the same regardless of the number of hours per day it is used, the average cost of the finished good declines as the volume of output increases. Thus large scales of operation are necessary if manufacturing is to be economically feasible. However, in order for large-scale output to be supported, a similarly large-scale market must exist; and here lies a major constraint for most developing countries – the local market is simply too small to support an economically efficient scale of manufacturing activity.

The import-substitution policies that many developing countries enacted have effectively stimulated local manufacturing, but the plants established are of less than optimum size. The finished goods produced in such plants are obviously high-cost items. Furthermore, as mentioned earlier in this chapter, the high-cost material inputs produced locally in other sub-scale plants further augment production costs in developing countries.

The G.S.P. is one policy which is aimed at alleviating the economic problems associated with small markets. A liberal G.S.P. (as opposed to the G.S.P. which exists) would provide large-scale (world) markets, thereby making it economically feasible for developing-country producers to construct plants of optimum size; but even with a liberal G.S.P., the problem of high-cost material inputs remains.

Another solution to the small-market problem is to enlarge the market by economic integration. After the Second World War the countries of Western Europe successfully formed two unified trading blocs – the European Economic Community and the European Free Trade Area. The effective market for any particular nation's producer was thus enlarged to include all countries belonging to that nation's trading bloc. Several such integration steps have been taken by groups of developing countries with limited degrees of success. The problems are many, ranging from purely monetary constraints caused by shortages of foreign exchange to disagreements concerning the industrial structures of the partner countries. Even with regional integration among developing countries, the market size is often so limited that only one or two optimal-scale manufacturing plants can be supported. In such cases the countries must negotiate the location of these plants. Such negotiations often de-emphasise the economic considerations for efficient resource allocation and instead highlight national prestige factors, for example every country wants its own steel mill, national airline, agricultural-machinery producer, high-technology petro-chemical plant, and so on. There are also fears that the natural allocation of smaller industries will be biased in favour of the more advanced countries in each bloc.

Even with these problems, we can be sure that the developing countries will be increasingly successful in building their regional groups and in deriving mutual economic benefit from them. Progress is likely to be slow and uneven, but nevertheless progress will occur.

Another approach which has received only minor attention would be a loose preference system among all developing countries. The degree of preferential treatment is much less important than the decision to actively promote trade among the developing countries. Today developing countries often *discriminate against* products produced in other developing countries. The present author recently had an opportunity to discuss such problems with numerous Western-based multinational corporations which have production facilities in developing countries. Most companies reported that when a particular developing-country importer was given the choice of importing a manufactured product produced in a near-by developing country or an equal product produced in the home-base developed country, the importer invariably chose the developed-country source. In a particular case, the multinational corporation went to great lengths to document that the output from the plant located in the near-by developing country was thoroughly tested for quality standards in the home-country laboratories and that the product met the same standards as the home-country product. The developing-country importer still chose the home-country product even though the quality standards were no better and, due to transport-cost differences, the landed import price was higher. If such discrimination against developing-country exports of manufactured products produced in multinational corporate plants exists, the degree of discrimination against developing-country exports from local entity plants must be very great indeed.

Such discriminatory treatment against developing-country sources of developing-country imports of manufactured products would seem to be a rather easy problem to correct. Furthermore, an agreement among the members of the Group of 77 to actively promote trade in manufactures among developing countries would also seem rather easy to reach, especially since neither of these agreements would impose a cost on any developing country. To carry this one step forward to the introduction of a G.S.P.-type preferential system would involve some costs in the form of administrative resources, tariff revenue forgone by importing governments, and the possibility of import displacement of local production. Of course the degree of these costs would depend upon the magnitude of the preference granted.

Another item that might further stimulate trade among developing countries would be the creation of some type of soft-currency payments settlements bank. The main purpose of establishing such a soft-currency settlements bank would be to eliminate foreign-exchange shortages as a barrier to intra-developing-country trade. One would suspect that the most effective stimulus to trade among the developing countries would come from active measures to promote such trade rather than any preferential treatment favouring developing-country sources of imports or from credit facilities provided by a developing countries' settlements bank.

But more importantly, these programmes to expand trade among developing countries can be pursued and negotiated independently of the developed countries. In contrast, the other elements of the 'new international economic order' can only be achieved in co-operation with the industrial nations.

Trade in primary commodities

Whereas the recent international pressure for an 'Integrated Programme for Commodities' is new, the attention devoted to commodity markets is not. The developing countries have repeatedly emphasised since the 1950s that their prospects for economic development were hampered because of undependable world markets for their commodity exports. This problem was of paramount importance for many developing countries which depended upon commodity exports for the bulk of their foreign-exchange earnings.

To the developing countries, international commodity markets possess two detrimental features: (1) in the short run commodity prices tend to fluctuate widely, causing substantial annual swings in the foreign-exchange earnings of developing countries; and (2) over the longer period the prices which developing countries receive for their commodity exports tend to decline relative to the prices they pay to developed countries for imports of manufactured products. The empirical evidence definitely supports the first allegation – that commodity prices fluctuate widely over the short run. However, the long-run price-trend evidence is not so conclusive. But regardless of the actual price trend, the developing countries' twofold concern – a concern for the *dependability* and *level* of their foreign-exchange earnings – is genuine.

The developing countries argue that the problem of dependability would be solved if the prices of their commodity exports were to be stabilised – through the establishment of commodity buffer stocks. Second, the level of their foreign-exchange earnings could be increased if the 'buffer-supported' prices received for their commodity exports were to be substantially raised from current levels.

There is little doubt about the ability of well-financed buffer stock programmes to stabilise commodity prices. The only question is the size of the necessary financial resources. However, buffer stocks cannot stabilise prices *and* guarantee a long-run price above the market-clearing price unless the financial resources are unlimited and are used to build ever-increasing stockpiles. Long-run price increases require cartel-type action (whether under private, government or international sanctions) which controls production and allocates sales among the various producing units (companies or countries). Finally, since any internationally created buffer-stock programme is certain to have finite financial resources, increasing the long-term price of commodities is not certain to increase the foreign-exchange earnings derived from commodity exports. Prices are invariably tied to sales volume; as price rises volume declines and the total receipts may increase or decrease – it all depends on the market.

The effectiveness of such an international programme for commodities faces other problems as well. It must be recognised that developing-country exporters are generally only minor suppliers of the commodities which they export; they supply less than one-quarter of the world production of the commodities covered by UNCTAD's 'Integrated Programme for Commodities'. Therefore, the success of any buffer-stock programme depends crucially on the response of the developed-country producers, who account for the other three-quarters of world production. At the very least, a price-stabilisation programme will guarantee the economic viability of the developed-country output from existing marginal production facilities – facilities that might otherwise be phased out of production as new, more efficient, facilities are created in the developing countries; and any international programme to increase commodity prices would stimulate increased production from these marginal facilities in developed countries, thereby supplying a larger share of the domestic market and reducing the demand for internationally traded commodities. Increased commodity prices would also stimulate increased efforts to develop synthetic substitutes for natural commodities.

These types of problems are recognised. In addition to stable and increased price levels, the developing countries call for commodity purchase and sale commitments by governments to establish the volume of commodity trade; but such commitments are likely to meet much resistance from the developed countries. There is no way that developed-country governments can provide guaranteed markets for developing-country commodities that simultaneously impose restrictions on domestic producers of competing (natural and synthetic) commodities.

Whenever one thinks about an international programme for commodities, the following question arises: Why tie up commodity markets when there is such a simple alternative? The primary objective of the programme is: (1) to assure developing countries of a minimum level of foreign-exchange earnings (via stabilised commodity prices); and (2) to provide a financial transfer from developed to developing countries (via increased commodity prices). The first objective could be provided by a programme along the lines of the STABEX facility of the E.E.C. Lomé Convention. This facility essentially finances (via loans or grants) a developing country's shortfall in its earnings derived from commodity exports to the E.E.C. But why should foreign-exchange earning shortfalls be financed only when the developing country is having problems with commodity exports? Why not instead have a general programme to cover all shortfalls in foreign-exchange earnings regardless of the cause? Are commodity exporters more deserving or worthy of multilateral assistance than other developing countries? It is hoped that they are not. Besides, just such a general foreign-exchange earnings support programme does exist – the I.M.F. Compensatory Financing Facility. It seems more reasonable to improve and expand this facility than to create a new programme that will help only those developing countries that export commodities while ignoring the others.*

The second objective of increasing the financial resources of developing countries via increasing commodity prices makes even less sense. The world understands very well the implications of changing the international prices of commodities – OPEC saw to that. Does one really believe that the developing countries can 'trick' the citizens of the world into granting financial transfers through commodity pricing that they are unwilling to grant through direct-aid-type transfers? And why should these resource transfers be allocated among the developing countries in proportion to their ability to export commodities? It is very unlikely that such an allocation would correspond to that dictated by economic need or by the ability to efficiently utilise additional resources. And what about those developing countries that do not have commodities to export? We should also realise that three-quarters of the transfer via commodities will go to the developed-country producers. Finally, we must not forget that some of the 'transferring' importers of commodities are also developing countries. Remember the countries that suffered the most (and are still suffering) from the OPEC oil price hike; most are developing countries. In summary, using commodity price increases as a mechanism to transfer financial resources has the following consequences: (1) it will primarily benefit developed-country producers; (2) the benefit which does accrue to developing countries will be shared according to the ability to export commodities rather than according to need or the ability to use it; and (3) the importing countries most likely to suffer are developing countries.

If the UNCTAD 'Integrated Programme for Commodities' is established, it is to be feared that the final outcome will cause more problems than it solves. Extreme political pressure is to be expected to be exerted by the developing countries to continually increase the buffer-support price, thus creating more and more incentives for users to search for substitutes, synthetic or otherwise. And once synthetic substitutes are found, they generally possess characteristics that make them more desirable than the former natural products. The following scenario can be envisaged. As a particular commodity price is increased, a synthetic substitute is developed. The synthetic substitute becomes more widely used to the point that commodity producers reassess their pricing policy. However, the users find that the synthetic material is cleaner, neater and more efficient, and consequently

* On the other hand, one might justify stabilising commodity prices to improve the long-term prospects for commodity production and marketing. It is possible that price fluctuations (rather than price levels) may cause some users to switch to more stable-priced synthetic alternatives. Stable prices may also reduce supply problems by improving the climate for investment in new and improved production capacity.

continue to use the synthetic even after the price relationship is reversed, making the natural product available at a price lower than the newly introduced synthetic substitute. An entire market for a particular commodity is lost. Moral: policy mistakes, once made, may not be reversible.

In contrast, the G.S.P. is a programme that provides developing countries with a slight marginal benefit of preferred access to developed-country markets which is superimposed on top of most-favoured-nation access. If the developing countries treat the G.S.P. as such, and nothing more, the G.S.P. will provide some benefit without creating any harm. On the other hand, if the G.S.P. is considered an end in itself, and the developing countries pursue policies to protect their preferred position by sabotaging future reductions in M.F.N. tariff and non-tariff barriers, they may very well end up worse off. The developing countries must not forget that in many areas they are competitive on an international level; improved access on an M.F.N. basis would be more beneficial than their restricted access under the G.S.P. However, unlike the G.S.P., the current negotiations for an international commodities programme is full of opportunities to cause real hardship to developing countries. An ill-designed programme may cause permanent damage to the export prospects for particular commodities, especially if these programmes call for substantial increases in commodity prices.

THE FUTURE: CONFRONTATION OR CO-OPERATION?

The first negotiations toward a 'new international economic order' really began in 1964 with the convening of UNCTAD I, which eventually led to the introduction of the G.S.P. in 1971. This first meeting was nothing more than a confrontation between North and South. The South demanded concessions which would benefit them; the North sought but could not find mutual benefit. The conference ended without agreement on any substantive issue.

During the intervening years little of substance has emerged, although the developed countries have made it look good by occasionally conceding on a few items; but as shown by the G.S.P. example, when a programme with no mutual benefit is agreed upon, it is coupled with sufficient loop-holes such that it also has little benefit for the developing countries. In the jargon of GATT, no reciprocity, no concession.

But what should one expect to emerge from a confrontation? A confrontation arises when interdependent parties have inconsistent objectives. The rich prefer to continue the present system, which the poor contend places them at a disadvantage; the poor argue for a new system, which the rich contend will come only at their expense. But we might ask what is so unique about rich–poor relations? All international economic problems arise because one party perceives itself to be at some kind of a disadvantage. The distinction arises when we consider the alternative solutions which apply in all confrontation cases:

(1) a solution is agreed upon through reconciliation of competing objectives based on mutual benefit – each party grants one concession in return for another; or

(2) a solution is imposed by one party on the other as a result of having a special position of power.

In the first case the problem goes away for both parties but in the second it remains for the weaker party.

So the essence of the answer to the question – confrontation or co-operation? – depends upon the opportunities for mutual benefit through reconciliation. As long as the developing countries continue to call for non-reciprocal concessions, the solution via economic power is likely to result; and the pure economic power possessed by the developing countries is limited indeed – regardless of what one might think in the aftermath of the OPEC experience. Instead the developing countries should pursue policies which hold out the prospects for mutual benefit. Although pure economic power may be lacking, the opportunities for mutually beneficial agreement abound.

Under the confrontation situation, developing countries threaten to withhold their raw materials from world markets. While such embargoes have limited long-run impacts (due to the possibilities of substitution and, of course, reverse embargoes on food and medicine), they do have serious short-run adjustment effects. Thus the developing countries do have a concession to grant, namely 'guaranteed access to material supplies'. This might be offered in return for commodity price-stabilisation programmes and/or the elimination of tariff-escalation discouragements against developing-country processors of locally available raw materials; and the developing countries have growing markets which are currently heavily protected by high import-substitution tariffs. Improved access to these markets could be exchanged for improved access to developed-country markets for labour-intensive products such as textiles, shoes, toys, sporting goods, plywood and veneer, and so on. Also, a more constructive tone during international negotiations would substantially increase the probability of increased aid flows from North to South.

But in the final analysis, the initiatives taken on the international front, even with co-operation from the developed countries, will have a minor impact in comparison to the job that needs to be done. The major benefits will be derived from measures taken within the developing countries themselves – measures that these nations have the power to implement with or without international co-operation. These are measures that must be taken before the developing countries can significantly accelerate their rates of economic growth, with or without international programmes of assistance. Progress begins at home.

Notes and References

CHAPTER 1

1. For a more detailed treatment, see UNCTAD, *Towards a New Trade Policy for Development* (the Prebisch Report) Report of the Secretary-General to the U.N. Conference on Trade and Development (New York: United Nations, 1964).

2. *Trends in International Trade*, A Report by a Panel of Experts (Geneva: GATT, 1958).

3. A detailed discussion of these issues is contained in B. Gosovic, *UNCTAD: Conflict and Compromise* (Leiden: Sijthoff, 1972).

4. The provisions and their impacts on preferential trading are covered in some detail in Part 2 (see Chapters 3–7).

CHAPTER 2

1. A note for academic readers; this rather simplistic analysis of the welfare effects of tariff preferences ignores a number of theoretical qualifications, such as distinguishing final goods from intermediates, substitution effects, supply constraints, non-competitive pricing behaviour, and so on. My justification is that I do not wish to interrupt the reader with these static details, which are generally considered to be of minor importance compared to dynamic considerations. Besides, these qualifications are well covered elsewhere in the literature; see, for example, H. G. Johnson, *Aspects of the Theory of Tariffs* (Harvard University Press, 1971).

2. This point, as well as others favouring tariff preferences, are brought out in H. G. Johnson, *Economic Policies Toward Less Developed Countries* (Washington, D.C.: Brookings Institution, 1967) ch. VI.

3. United Nations, *World Economic Survey*, 1962, Part II (New York: United Nations, 1963).

4. For example, see B. Balassa, 'Tariff Protection in Industrial Countries: An Evaluation', *Journal of Political Economy*, Dec. 1965; 'The Impact of the Industrial Countries' Tariff Structure on Their Imports of Manufactures from Less-Developed Areas', *Economica*, Nov 1967; and 'Tariff Protection in Industrial Nations and Its Effects on the Exports of Processed Goods From Developing Countries', *Canadian Journal of Economics*, Aug 1968.

5.   These estimates were given in confidence by a multinational corporate official as representative of his firm's situation. If the developing-country exporter sells through an export–import relationship, rather than being a multinational corporation, the import costs would be calculated as that part of the importer's mark-up which is in excess of normal domestic distributor mark-ups – in all likelihood a figure more in the range of 50 per cent than 10 per cent. Transport costs ranging from 3 to 39 per cent and averaging 10 per cent were found by J. M. Finger and A. J. Yeats, 'Effective Protection by Transportation Costs and Tariffs: A Comparison of Magnitudes', *Quarterly Journal of Economics*, Feb 1976.

6.   B. Balassa and Associates, *The Structure of Protection in Developing Countries* (Baltimore: Johns Hopkins Press, 1971).

7.   Johnson, *Economic Policies Toward Less Developed Countries*, pp. 174–5.

8.   *Ibid.* pp. 178–9.

CHAPTER 3

1.   *Journal of Commerce*, 14 May 1975.

2.   Report of the House Committee on Ways and Means, *Trade Reform Act of 1973*, 93d Congress, 1st Session, House Report No. 93–571, pp. 84–5.

3.   This figure applies to the initial twenty-one Associates under the Yaoundé and Arusha agreements; see UNCTAD, *Operation and Effects of the Generalized System of Preferences*, document TD/B/C.5/15, p. 65.

4.   The United Nations recognises the following twenty-five countries as least developed: in Africa Botswana, Burundi, Chad, Dahomey, Ethiopia, Guinea, Lesotho, Malawi, Mali, Niger, Rwanda, Somalia, Sudan, Uganda, Tanzania, and the Upper Volta; in Asia and Oceania Afghanistan, Bhutan, Laos, the Maldive islands, Nepal, Sikkim and Western Samoa; in Latin America Haiti; and in the Middle East the Yemen. For details see the Report of the Committee for Development Planning, 7th Session *Official Records of the Economic and Social Council*, 51st Session, Supplement No. 7, E/4990, ch. II.

CHAPTER 6

1.   *The Trade Act of 1974*, section 503(b).

2.   UNIDO, *Profiles of Manufacturing Establishments* (New York: United Nations, 1971) vol. III.

CHAPTER 7

1.   This section is based on R. E. Baldwin and T. Murray, 'MFN Tariff Reductions and Developing Country Trade Benefits Under the GSP', *Economic Journal*, Mar 1977.

2.   A survey of estimation methods and results is contained in M. E. Kreinin, 'Effects of the EEC on Imports of Manufactures', *Economic Journal*, Sep 1972.

3.   The elasticities were taken from M. Buckler and C. Almond, 'Import and Export in an Input–Output Model', *American Statistical Association Proceedings*, 1972; and S. Magee, 'Prices, Incomes, and Foreign Trade', Conference on Research in International Trade and Finance, Princeton University, 30–1 Mar 1973, reprinted in *International Trade and Finance: Frontiers for Research*, ed. P. Kenen (Cambridge University Press, 1975).

4.   U.S. production data were obtained from U.S. Bureau of the Census, *U.S. Commodity Exports and Imports as Related to Output, 1971 and 1970* (Washington, D.C.: U.S. Government Printing Office, 1974). Ratios of imports from non-beneficiaries to E.E.C. production were obtained from E.E.C. *Tableaux Entrees-Sorties 1965*. Ratios for Japan were calculated from the 1965 sixty-six-sector Japanese input–output table.

5.   See R. E. Baldwin, *Nontariff Distortions of International Trade* (Washington, D.C.: Brookings Institution, 1970).

6.   I. Walter and J. Chung, 'Non-tariff Distortions and Trade Preferences for Developing Countries', *Kyklos*, fasc. 4, 1971.

CHAPTER 9

1.   This section is based on R. E. Baldwin and T. Murray, 'MFN Tariff Reductions and Developing Country Trade Benefits Under the GSP', *Economic Journal*, Mar 1977.

CHAPTER 10

1.   J. M. Finger, 'GATT Tariff Concessions and the Exports of Developing Countries – U.S. Concessions at the Dillon Round', *Economic Journal*, Sep 1974; and 'Effects of the Kennedy Round Tariff Concessions on the Exports of Developing Countries', *Economic Journal*, Mar 1976.

2.   J. M. Finger, 'Tariff Provisions for Offshore Assembly and the Exports of Developing Countries', *Economic Journal*, June 1975; see also U.S. Tariff Commission, *Economic Factors Affecting the Use of Items 807.00 and 806.30 of the Tariff Schedules of the United States*, TC Publication 339, Sep 1970.

3.   B. Balassa and Associates, *The Structure of Protection in Developing Countries* (Baltimore: Johns Hopkins Press, 1971).

Bibliography

PART 1

B. GOSOVIC, *UNCTAD: Conflict and Compromise* (Leiden: Sijthoff, 1972).

H. G. JOHNSON, *Economic Policies Toward Less Developed Countries* (Washington, D.C.: Brookings Institution, 1967).

R. KRISHNAMURTI, 'Tariff Preferences in Favour of the Developing Countries', *Journal of World Trade Law*, Nov–Dec 1967 and May–June 1970.

P. TULLOCH, *The Politics of Preferences* (London: Overseas Development Institute, 1975).

UNCTAD, *Towards a New Trade Policy for Development* (the Prebisch Report), Report of the Secretary-General to the U.N. Conference on Trade and Development (New York: United Nations, 1964).

PART 2

R. COOPER, 'The European Community's System of Generalized Tariff Preferences: A Critique', *Journal of Development Studies*, July 1972.

J. M. FINGER, 'The Generalized Scheme of Preferences: Impact on the Donor Countries', *Bulletin of Economic Research*, May 1973.

B. HINDLEY, 'The UNCTAD Agreement on Preferences', *Journal of World Trade Law*, Nov–Dec 1971.

Z. IQBAL, 'Trade Effects of the Generalized System of Preferences', *International Monetary Fund Departmental Memoranda*, DM/75/31, Apr 1975.

UNCTAD, *Operation and Effects of the Generalized System of Preferences*, selected studies submitted to the Fifth and Sixth Sessions of the Special Committee on Preferences, Geneva, 3–13 Apr 1973 and 20–31 May 1974, documents TD/B/C.5/15 and TD/B/C.5/42.

———— *Operation and Effects of the Scheme of Generalized Preferences of the European Economic Community: Study of the Operation of the Scheme in 1972*, document TD/B/C.5/34 and addendum 1.

———— *Scheme of Generalized Preferences of the United States of America*, document TD/B/C.5/38 and addendum 1.

U.S. TARIFF COMMISSION, *Probable Effects of Tariff Preferences for Developing Countries* (Washington, D.C.: U.S. Tariff Commission, 1972).

PART 3

B. BALASSA and ASSOCIATES, *The Structure of Protection in Developing Countries* (Baltimore: Johns Hopkins Press, 1971).

R. E. BALDWIN and T. MURRAY, 'MFN Tariff Reductions and Developing Country Trade Benefits Under the GSP', *Economic Journal*, Mar 1977.

P. COFFEY, *The External Economic Relations of the EEC* (London: Macmillan, 1976).

M. E. KREININ and J. M. FINGER, 'A New International Economic Order? (A Critical Survey of the Issues)', *Journal of World Trade Law*, Nov–Dec 1976.

UNCTAD, *A Comprehensive Policy for Strengthening and Diversifying the Exports of Developing Countries in Manufactures and Semi-Manufactures*, document TD/B/C.2/153, 1975.

—— *An Integrated Programme for Commodities*, document TD/B/C.1/166 and supplements 1–6, 1975.

—— *Effects of the Enlargement of the European Economic Community on the Generalized System of Preferences*, document TD/B/C.5/8; reprinted in *Operation and Effects of the Generalized System of Preferences*, Fifth Session, document TD/B/C.5/15, 1974.

—— *The Generalized System of Preferences and the Multilateral Trade Negotiations*, document TD/B/C.5/26; reprinted in *Operations and Effects of the Generalized System of Preferences*, Sixth Session, document TD/B/C.5/42, 1975.

Index